Mind Your Own Business

Neither this book, nor most of the things in my life of
which I am most proud, would have been possible
without the understanding, cooperation, support, and
wisdom of my father, Sy Syms.

MIND YOUR OWN BUSINESS

And Keep It in the Family

MARCY SYMS

MASTERMEDIA LIMITED
New York

Library of Congress Cataloging-in-Publication Data

Syms, Marcy.
Mind your own business : and keep it in the family / Marcy Syms.
p. cm.
ISBN 0-942361-46-6
1. Family-owned business enterprises—Management. 2. Success in business. I. Title.
HD62.25.S96 1992
658.02′2–dc20 92-35588
CIP

Production services by Martin Cook Associates, Ltd., New York
Manufactured in the United States of America
10 9 8 7 6 5 4 3 2 1

This book is dedicated to
my family team players,
Stephen, Robert, and Adrienne

Contents

Contents

Acknowledgments

Seventy-five members of 34 family businesses shared the experiences and dreams of their family enterprises with me in the hope that others might profit. To all of them—founders, successors, and nonfamily employees—my heartfelt thanks. Perhaps those who are helped by reading this book will also thank you.

Ethan Allen Franchise, Omaha, Nebraska

American Life & Accident Insurance Company of Kentucky, Louisville

Black Enterprise Magazine, New York

Brownstone Studios, New York

Carlson Companies, Inc., Minneapolis

Castro Convertibles, New Hyde Park, New York

Claire's Boutiques, Inc., New York

Drown Publishing, Los Angeles

Durkin & Durkin, Newark

Echo Design Group, New York

Acknowledgments

Edelman Public Relations Worldwide, Chicago/New York

Salvatore Ferragamo, New York

Frieda's Finest Produce Specialties, Inc., Los Angeles

Norman Hilton Apparel, Linden, New Jersey

HMK Group Companies, Inc., Waltham, Massachusetts

H&R Block, Kansas City, Missouri

Inner-City Broadcasting Corporation, New York

Georgette Klinger, Inc., Los Angeles/New York

Kohler & Company, Kohler, Wisconsin

Lefrak Organization, Inc., New York

Mansfield Industries, Mansfield, Ohio

Martha Inc. of New York, New York

Alice F. Mason, Ltd., New York

Henry Modell & Company, Inc., Long Island City

Pierre's French Ice Cream Company, Cleveland

Playboy Enterprises, Inc., Chicago

Procide Construction, Bronx, New York

Ruder Finn, Inc., New York

Rudin Management Company, Inc., New York

H. J. Russell & Company, Atlanta

Scott Magazine, Inc., New York

Acknowledgments

Sylvia's Restaurant, New York

Vose Galleries, Boston

The Weight Watchers Group, Inc., Farmington Hills, Michigan

And lastly, my deepest personal gratitude to a couple of people who hold a special place in my life, for surviving my obsession with the subject of family business—you are loved.

Mind Your Own Business

Introduction

One night during the winter of 1980, my father drove me home after we had both worked late at the Park Place store in New York City.

"By the way, Marcy," he said casually. "I'm going to be putting this in writing, but if something should happen to me, you'll be responsible. I hope you don't think that's too heavy a burden."

I was quite simply overwhelmed.

My father's need to name a successor arose because his doctors had recently advised him of a health problem. He realized he had to start thinking about the future of Syms, the off-price clothing retail company he had founded. At the time, four of his six children were working for Syms. The oldest male, my brother Stephen, was a buyer, reporting to Sy. Middle brother Robert was an assistant buyer, and my youngest brother, Richard—who viewed himself as the obvious heir apparent—was a store manager. My two sisters, the youngest children, had not started to work yet. I joined in 1978 after some outside work experience, learning the business from the switchboard up. By 1980, I had made good use of my outside experience and the caretaking skills learned over the years as the oldest child.

Three years later, when we sold part of the company in 1983 on the New York Stock Exchange, we worked with investment bankers and Wall Streeters who helped us organize our responsibilities by job titles. I became president of Syms, and a year later took on the additional responsibilities of chief operating officer. Once I was identified as president, and it was official, all hell broke loose. My brothers saw me as the usurper of their birthright. How dare I! *They* were the sons. After some ugly, painful confrontations, one of my brothers resigned, to be followed by another.

The Wall Street Journal had sent me a little plaque of the announcement that Syms had gone public on September 23, 1983. At thirty-two, I was one of the youngest woman corporate presidents of a New York Stock Exchange company. I would often look at that little plaque, think what it had cost me in peace of mind, and wonder if it had been worth it.

Statistics vary when we try to assess how important family businesses are to the economy of the United States. But most observers agree that the 13 million family controlled businesses in the country today produce at least 60 percent of our gross national product and employ approximately 50 million people. That's almost a fifth of the entire population. And if the estimate is accurate that about 90 percent of all businesses are either family controlled or influenced, then we can be certain that family businesses are fundamental to our economic well-being.

I have worked for my father's company for almost fifteen years. Today Syms operates twenty-nine off-price apparel stores in eighteen marketing areas. I've learned a lot about how businesses operate and how families function in a work environment, and how the two combine when a family enterprise is the employer.

I've been thinking about just what makes family businesses tick, or break down and stop, for a long time now. And I've been talking about it to my counterparts in other family businesses, and occasionally to the public. In 1987, I addressed my first audience as part of a lecture series. My topic: "How to Succeed in a Family Business." I was overwhelmed by the reaction from both the press and the audience. For days following the talk, I was besieged by phone calls from people in other family businesses asking for advice and wanting to share their stories.

I was intellectually invigorated by the response to my lecture, and challenged by the conversations that stemmed from it. I wanted to know more about the dynamics of other family businesses and perhaps share some of my ideas and observations with a larger audience.

I didn't want to focus on the families that had failed—the Binghams, the Johnsons, and all those other families whose court battles fascinated the public.

I wanted to talk with the families who had succeeded—with the mothers and fathers who had brought their children into the business and had made it work. There did seem to be some successful business families who were blessed with both riches and long-term family harmony. I wanted to find them and talk with them. How did they deal with such issues as succession, separation of home and work, emotional problems, in-laws, sibling rivalry, communication, and twenty-four-hours-on-call accountability?

I started my project the way I start most things—I dove in headfirst. My memberships in such support groups as the Young Presidents' Organization, the Committee of Two Hundred Women, Women's Forum, and Women in Family Owned Businesses were a great way to start collecting contacts.

I set out to interview a modest number of people in multigenerational families from different industries. One family led me to another and the number kept growing. As it grew, what had originally been planned as an anecdotal view of the state of the family business became a descriptive survey that could be quantified. By the time my interviewing was complete, I had met with forty-four family businesses, talked with sixty-six members of those businesses, and had supplementary information on about forty additional family members.

The businesses in my sampling ranged in size from those with just a few employees, like Alice Mason Ltd., an exclusive New York City real estate broker, to five *Fortune* 500 companies. Two of those were in the top forty, including number thirteen, Carlson Companies of Minnesota.

Fifteen of the businesses had gross revenues of $15 million to $500 million a year; four were in the $1 billion range; and two grossed below $500,000. Of the ten that were publicly traded, half wanted to take the company private again; and six companies, like my own family business, were publicly traded with the family controlling at least 50 percent of the stock.

In addition to personal interviews, I read all I could find about family businesses in such publications as *Family Business* magazine, *Fortune*, *The New York Times*, *Working Woman*, *Self*, and *Black Enterprise*. I was particularly fortunate to be able to interview several African American business families, including Earl Graves, *Black Enterprise* publisher; Percy Sutton of Inner City Broadcasting Corporation; Herman J. Russell, chairman of the construction and engineering firm H. J. Russell & Company; and the three-generation Woods family of the country's most famous soul-food restaurant, Sylvia's, in New York City's Harlem.

I was lucky to find families that had survived for several generations—very rare in the world of family businesses, in which only one in seven makes it to the third generation. I found five fourth-generation families and one that was into the fifth, the Vose family of Vose Gallery in Boston.

I interviewed big families like that of Robert Matt, who holds the numbers record for bringing six of his fourteen children into his family business, Ethan Allen and the Workbench. I interviewed small families, like mother-and-daughter skin-care and cosmetics executives Georgette and Kathryn Klinger. I met Florine Mark, of Weight Watchers in Detroit, who works with ten family members —five children, two sisters, her mother, a son-in-law, and a brother-in-law.

I had two criteria for inclusion in this descriptive survey: The businesses were to be multigenerational—that is, more than one generation actively participated in day-to-day operations; and they had to be successful. My definition of successful also was twofold: the business had to be doing well financially, and the family members should be relatively pleased with their role in the business. In my opinion, those that fit my definition were the sorts of functional families and companies I wanted to know. What did they have in common?

In all my interviews, I asked the same questions:

How do you separate your business and personal life? How do you deal with your parents' unwillingness to let go? How do you handle conflict? What are your rules for fighting fair? Are in-laws allowed or outlawed? Do you have outside board members, and how much power do they have? Do you have a mentor? What is the birth order in your family, and do you find it correlates with the role you play in the business? How did you enter the business, and under what circumstances? Did you first get experience elsewhere? What is unique about your family that helped you to beat the odds? What role does Mother play? And how do you deal with nepotism, croneyism, lack of privacy, squabbling siblings, burnout, and general loss of interest in the business by family members?

I had an additional interest—how did the women fare in these businesses, and what special problems did they face that their brothers did not?

The eleven chapters of this book deal with these questions. Although I have not mentioned all my respondents by name, it is their stories I am telling, as well as my own. As you will see there are problems, there are crises, there are conflicts. There are also no universal solutions. This book collects the best thinking that I could find and examines how different successful people handle the problems, crises and conflicts of both family and business. Whether you are a parent who wants to bring a child into the company, or a child considering the pros and cons, or the 50 percent of the working population employed by a family owned business, I hope that you find this book useful, interesting, and thought provoking. For family members in business together, I hope you take this book on a family business weekend retreat and see if it doesn't help you focus on some of the tough issues you face every day.

Chapter

1

Family Business:
An Oxymoron?

There are families and there are businesses, and then there are family businesses. Startlingly, 90 percent of all businesses are family owned or controlled. So it's no surprise that most of us work for such a company, either as a family member or as a non-related employee—or are thinking about joining one.

Are family businesses really different from the more widely held companies? I think they are. Each possess an ambiance that is the reflection of the family owning the company. Traditionally, the family business focuses more on people. Even very enlightened nonfamily companies will factor in the human equation only when it's demonstrably good for business. A sense of humanity may be simply too long-range a virtue to be attended to.

The internalized focus that humanizes family businesses does have a flip side. Inherently "family" and "business" are antithetical. Psychiatrist Roy Menninger, president of the renowned Menninger Foundation in Topeka, Kansas, explained: "Families have one set of purposes, businesses have another. Businesses presumably are created to perform a task or provide a service or make money—in a relatively impersonal manner to organize resources in a focused way.

"Families don't have that task at all. Their task is to create an environment of growth and to nurture and enable people to grow. In effect, grow up. In a way, a successful family is one that puts itself out of business. The children should be able to leave and form their own families."

Dr. Menninger's observations have been echoed by a host of business observers over the years. But it is possible for successful family businesses to adapt techniques of management that unite these contradictions in ways that play to their strengths.

What are those strengths? What are those characteristics that set family businesses apart and add to their appeal as a potential employer?

Most important is the ability of a family business to look to the future. Long-range planning is typical, as the founder/entrepreneur generally intends for his or her creation to go on and on and on.

Add to that job security for family and nonfamily members, and a family business begins to look like a cozy employment option. In addition, financial rewards may be substantial.

David Bork, an influential business consultant who founded the Bork Institute for Family Business at Aspen, Colorado, shared with me his notions of important family business qualities.

"These qualities are critical to ensuring success, profitability, and longevity of the family business, as well as the happiness, fulfillment, and future of the individual and the family unit," Bork said. He listed ten qualities, which, at least ideally, are more often found within family businesses than other sorts of companies:

1. Shared values
2. Shared power (what's fair is fair)
3. Shared traditions (the mortar that holds the family bricks together, I think)
4. Willingness to learn and grow (and problem-solve)
5. Fun activities together
6. Genuine caring
7. Mutual respect
8. Mutual assistance and support
9. Privacy
10. Well-defined interpersonal boundaries.

The above portrait gives you an idea of what you could find in a successful family business if you're fortunate. There are family businesses that are well run and could offer you most of the traits on Bork's list. If you're doubly fortunate, you might find them in your own family's business.

In this chapter, I would like to share with you some fundamental background about family businesses: what they are, where they came from, and a little of what they're like from the inside.

I know why I'm absorbed with the subject of family businesses in the United States—it's central to my life—and I also know why the person browsing in the business section of a bookstore might be interested. There's one chance in two that the browser is employed by a family owned or managed company. And it's simply good sense to try to understand a little about what makes a family business run smoothly, and of which pitfalls to be wary, whether you are a family member or an outside employee. It's realistic to protect your own self-interest.

We know that nine out of ten businesses in the United States are family dominated or family influenced. They employ between a third to one-half of all full-time workers. These companies may range in size from a local video franchise to the candymaker Mars, Inc., one of the most successful companies in the United States.

The feeling about joining one of these companies, whether or not you are a member of the family, has become even more positive as the country looks to the next century.

As Wendy C. Handler, professor of family business management at Babson College in Babson Park, Massachusetts, has noted, many workers, especially younger employees, are sick of the rigid bureaucracies and unyielding corporate culture frequently encountered in many of this country's megabusinesses. Also, fast-track corporate careers and fat salaries are no longer guaranteed along with a degree. New workers are stopping to smell the flowers in greater numbers than they did during the last frantic decade. There's a growing distaste for the workaholic ethos of the eighties.

There occasionally is a perception that in family companies the job seeker may find a more enlightened, humanistically oriented management, and greater opportunity for creativity in the workplace.

Sometimes these expectations are fulfilled and sometimes they are not, but a successful family enterprise may offer real advantages:

- *To nonfamily employees.*
  The nonfamily employee may be very handsomely paid in order to make up for his or her lack of equity in the company. In addition, that worker may find other compensations: freedom to create, flexibility in day-to-day routine, a customized benefits package, and job security if the company remains successful. The nonfamily member may be treated as if he or she were as much a part of the family as the blood relatives. You'll work just as hard as in a public company, but you'll have

a better chance of being recognized as an important business asset. The family couldn't fill your job from within its ranks. It had to go out and get you and then keep you satisfied.

- *To women.*

Women still have a tough time in corporate America. Conditions in the workplace have not changed as much as we once thought they would. Women, too, still have the children and, despite unquestionably more support and practical help from their mates, continue to do most of the housework and child-rearing. If a woman *is* a family member, *her* family business is one of the few organizations available to her in which she can rise to the top. And if a woman is not a family member, she may still find that the "family" atmosphere might offer greater understanding of the stress and time constraints that are no doubt her lot.

- *To family members.*

It's their family, and the founding generation usually wants them to succeed. And if that earlier generation has no murky hidden agenda, the new additions may find themselves with a real opportunity to do meaningful work.

- *To the community.*

Family businesses are often very concerned about their place in the community; they want to be good citizens. Corporate involvement could be literally anything, from day-care centers to neighborhood baseball games to fund raising—limited only by the creative energy and interests of the family and the success of the business.

THE POSTWAR ENTREPRENEURS

But will family businesses stay strong into the next generation? The end of World War II saw a commercial boom in this country. Returning servicemen, many of whom had learned all sorts of skills in the military, started hundreds of thousands of new businesses, and became the largest group of entrepreneurs in the history of the United States. Everything was in place for the entrepreneurial boom: cheap money, the availability of the GI Bill, inexpensive GI housing loans, and waiting markets here and overseas.

That generation was very successful, and many became CEOs of their own companies. But all this happened decades ago, and the business lives of that entrepreneurial generation are almost at an end. Most of those postwar business people are close to retirement or retired.

Which brings up two very big questions:

- Management succession and the passing of the torch from one generation to another.
- Ownership of assets so that the company can be passed through the tax laws intact following the death of the original shareholders. In a public company ownership is not inherited and therefore not taxable.

Because most companies have not faced these problems before, they are often not very expert in dealing with them. But they must not be ignored. No one wants to be employed by, or depend on financially, a company that may not survive the death of the founder because of poor financial planning, with no future management in place.

As the entrepreneurial generation ages, and perhaps stagnates, heirs are scrambling to protect their own interests. Some founders are surprised to find their children eyeing the family business with new interest. The children see the need to preserve their assets, even if they do not work for the company.

According to David R. Hoods of the Geneva Company's Marketing Sciences Division, one-half of his business-owning clients between the ages of fifty-two and sixty want to retire soon. Perhaps they're bored or burned out or just want to enjoy some years in the sun. Two-thirds of these clients have children anxious to take over the family business—a big surprise to many of the parents, who are often eager to pass on their business legacy but have been rejected in the past.

One explanation for this turnaround is that the children of the Baby Boom, who once spurned any idea of going into the family firm, are now taking a hard second look at what they once passed over. *Inc. Magazine*'s Curtis Hartman commented: "To this anti-establishment generation, Big Business has always been Bad Business. But family business, once disparaged as narrow and bourgeois, appeals to other cherished values: closeness to the consumer, loyalty to employees, independence for managers and owners. The wallflower is becoming the belle of the ball."

For those young workers who perhaps already have had a go-round with a large corporation and experienced reorganization, cutbacks, or been mega-mergered out of a job, the family business, if one exists, presents an attractive career alternative.

LIVING BETWEEN PARALLEL SYSTEMS

To many, and I count myself among them, the family business supplies a challenging environment in which to develop career goals and personal growth. But it's not exactly an easy way of life. What about fourteen-hour days? And the stress of being ultimately responsible for the financial future of your family?

Then there's the physical daily presence of one or many members of your family, which may be a mixed blessing. You cannot, for example, leave family problems at home and lose yourself in your work. Those family problems might be sitting right across the hall in the physical presence of a brother with whom you've never gotten along. Or a business crisis that you've all been agonizing about at the office for days could pop up like an unwanted guest at a family picnic.

"According to psychologists," said family business consultant Benjamin Benson in *Your Family Business*, "family and business can each be viewed as systems that define people by their relationships with others in the same environment, rather than as individuals.

"The family system is emotionally based, with emphasis on loyalty and the care and nurturing of family members, while the business system is task-based, with emphasis on performance and results rather than on the emotional considerations of family life. Is it any wonder that when these two basically incompatible systems overlap, as they do in a family business, there is conflict?"

And is it any wonder that unless strong, effective systems are put in place to handle conflict, jealousy, stress, disagreement, pride, and any of the other sins that members of a family business might be heir to, each generation in the family business runs the risk of being the last generation? In fact, those of us in a family business hear all too often that:

- Two out of three entrepreneurs fail to establish a business successful enough to pass on to the second generation.
- Of those family businesses that succeed, only one in seven survives beyond the second generation.

• Of that group, only one in ten lasts beyond the third generation.

Most of the second-generation family members that I spoke with agreed that the operative word in "family business" is "business." If family conflict is allowed to get in the way of business as usual, then the whole house of cards runs the risk of collapsing. Clearly, the newly adult children coming into the company must leave their childish toys behind them, and function as loyal employees doing real work.

This is not so easy in practice. After all, that's *your* daddy, or mommy, sitting behind the door that says "CEO." And you have a long history with that person.

When I joined the family business I didn't realize how many demons I would have to face, although I was clear about what my commitment would be: total immersion and hard work. I decided to talk to a therapist to try to understand in a more objective way what my relationship with my parents really was, as well as to identify the emotional baggage I needed to leave behind and find out what useful traits I had within myself on which I could build. How could I best fulfill the dual role of child and employee?

One of the basics that you learn in therapy is that you can't change the behavior of others. But you *can* change your own, and if you do, those others will have to respond to you in a different way. Rearranging behavior patterns is fundamental to growth, and one of the hardest things in the world to do is to achieve a comfortable level of interaction.

In my case, I learned to become less of a caretaker. I learned to understand that I was not responsible for the happiness of my brothers and sisters. There were other hard truths to learn. There were going to be times, for instance, when I wouldn't meet the approval of my father, and when an increasingly successful relationship with him would cause tension with my mother, who, because they were divorced, felt angry and alienated.

Every family history is complicated, with some animosities and even alliances lost in the mists of early memory. But crises stemming from changes in relationships are what test the boundaries of love and understanding among people.

I knew that my search for understanding was complicated by my joining my father's company. This was a fundamental change in my work life, and it was bound to have some effect on my family relationships. I knew that I would have to find new ways of dealing with these changing relationships.

But families spend decades establishing their communication patterns—the way a father speaks to his son, the way a father speaks to a daughter, a wife to her husband, a sister to her brother. These old behavior patterns, instinctive as breathing, are almost impossible to break unless they are identified and analyzed. It does help to have a therapist or consultant, free from the coils of your family bonds, recognize and help you to understand preconceived ideas, unfair assumptions based on past behavior long outgrown, and to assist in developing new ways of communication that are neither threatening nor defensive.

A Search For Understanding

Once I had made a commitment to our family firm, I realized that I wanted to know a lot more about what made us do the things we did, and how we stacked up against other family businesses in confronting our problems, both business and personal. I wanted answers because I felt overwhelmed by my dual role. When I was appointed president, I not only had to hone my managerial skills, but also had to deal with my dad, who was the founder. I believed then, as I do now, that the more I knew about processes within other family concerns, the more effective I would be at Syms.

Therefore, I began a process of self-education about a subject for which there was then no formal, systematized curriculum. I began a clippings file of everything I read in magazines and newspapers about family business and taped television shows featuring family members discussing how they managed business and personal conflicts. I enrolled in family business seminars and workshops, spoke to consultants, and had a lot of heart-to-heart discussions with my peers.

Once I started to look, I found that there were a lot of people out there whose problems were similar to my own. I became a member of the Young Presidents' Organization, 40 percent of whose membership are presidents of their own family controlled businesses, and found new friends. I expanded my circle by joining the Committee of 200, a group of women entrepreneurs, as well as Women in Family Owned Businesses, which was developed as an outgrowth of the Family Business Program at the University of Pennsylvania. Like me, other members of these groups were seeking a network within which to exchange war stories and give support, feedback, and validation.

As I've noted, families traditionally function in an atmosphere of cooperation and meeting emotional needs, whereas businesses function in an atmosphere of competition and logic. As I talked with dozens of family business members, it became clear that if the two systems are successfully combined, the environment created is emotionally satisfying to those involved. For example, nontraditional male-female roles are enhanced, with the men learning to become more nurturing and the women more assertive. Companies combining these two systems are flexible and can somehow extract the best from each member. It is here that employees with different personalities, interests, and talents can find their niches.

Is the description above too good to be true—too good to be real? Some companies do come closer to that ideal than others. How do they do it? I think that the secret is in recognizing that cooperation, confidence, and creativity are assets, and rewarding employees who exhibit such traits. In other words, taking the best of *family* behavior and making it work for the family business. And to cooperation, confidence, and creativity I would add a fourth "c" —compromise, surely a necessity in any working relationship, even if you're the boss.

American companies now have to compete internationally, as well as struggle at home for a shrinking pool of capable employees. The uncontrolled rush to leveraged companies and the merger mania of the eighties are dead and unlamented. We're entering a time in business when cooperation, within and without a company, is going to become necessary to survive.

Cooperation and compromise, two of our five "c"s, form the underpinnings of the most successful corporate cultures that I know. The presence of these two traits assures mutual attention to feelings, and free discussion of differing attitudes and opinions. That's how you create the shared goals that are necessary if the company is to pay good attention to business.

I think this is the harbinger of things to come, and cooperative techniques will have to be adopted in most fields, including the one I know best, the family firm. Smart businesses don't buck new ways of thinking that seem to work. Tradition is all very well, but family businesses, like all commercial enterprises, must remain open to new ideas so they can adopt those that fit well into their corporate structure. The fifth "c," communication, is at the bottom of all change that works. New ideas have to be discussed, in straightforward debate, with open minds, in a language that every member of the family business understands.

THE PULL OF
THE FAMILY BUSINESS

The trend toward entrepreneurship and the desire to control one's own destiny reflect a great prevailing social need to fill the void caused by the 50 percent divorce rate and the fundamental changes in business markets. People long to feel connected to something larger than themselves. Well-run family businesses are an ideal replacement for the extended family that many people have lost or have never known but for which they yearn. Kate Ludeman, who writes about organizations, said, "The demographics of the work force have changed so much that many people have no one at home to count on. They look to work to fill that vacuum."

Life in the United States today is much less centered and stable than it used to be a generation or two ago. Women are in the workforce, and not tending to the hearth; the extended family rarely exists, with parents living in a Sun Belt condominium rather than in the house next door; and economic uncertainty abounds. We are in an unstable cultural era right now, both personally and economically, and I think that it's true that many Americans do look to the workplace for a sense of family and identity.

One CEO describes his successful family firm as being "run positively to allow for personal development of individuals. Healthy families, like healthy businesses, are supportive rather than critical, rewarding rather than punitive, truthful rather than secret, and foster interdependency and a feeling of being valuable."

One of the most attractive aspects of family businesses is the presence of old-fashioned values of loyalty, commitment, and continuity. These are important to people, especially if they lack them in their personal lives. "When the chips are down, there is great security and power in knowing that your flank is protected," said Peter Glazer, a management consultant for family businesses. And many people can find that security in a family business.

There is a kind of immortality that can be found by those lucky enough to enjoy a positive relationship with a viable, continuing family business. If that business continues to be successful, it can furnish family members with a satisfying sense of connection across generational boundaries. Family patriarch J. Dinwiddie Lampton, Jr., a Lexington, Kentucky, second-generation president of a three-generation family run insurance company, shared this thought: "Being in a family business gives us an idea that we're part of the flow of generations, so we don't think of ourselves only in terms of our lifetime. We connect back and we connect in the future. That's basic to civilized life, a social life, and without a generational sense we're lost as a civilization."

I started the research for this book because I wanted to know firsthand what made successful family companies work, what they had in common. Since those early days several years ago, the subject of what makes a family business function well has attracted the interest of consultants, journalists, writers, and academics. Most agree that a well-functioning family unit has a better chance to manage a successful family business. In my search for both truths and workable solutions to problems, I have benefitted from many of their observations.

Sharon Nelton, the senior editor of *Nation's Business*, is one expert who has been studying family businesses in order to uncover common behavioral traits that work. Nelton commented, "The more I see of family businesses that function well, the more I realize how much they have to teach the rest of us about living as families. Perhaps the family is so strong to begin with that anything they tried would succeed. Possibly it's because they use some of the techniques and skills learned in the business to manage their personal relationships. If you can learn to translate these business skills into the family, you can learn to have a better family unit."

Another expert on family businesses who has come to the same conclusion is consultant Barbara Hollander. She has described a successful combining of the family and business systems as two intertwined circles with dotted lines in the area in which they overlap. If there is harmony within the dotted lines, there's success on the bottom line as well. "Without exception," said Hollander, "in the work I've done in the past few years, if you've got a healthy family you will have a well-functioning business."

As I spoke with those seventy-five members of successful family businesses who were trying to help me pinpoint business and personal traits that seemed universal to good management and self-satisfaction, I identified several themes quite easily—they appeared again and again. Some are described often in the growing literature on family businesses—they are, after all, truisms. Other results of my survey were unexpected, and a surprise both to me and to my interviewees, as we discussed some previously unrecognized similarities in both our experiences.

For example, one of the most startling results of my research was discovering how many second-generation families replicated Syms' pattern of greatly increased volume once the children and parents worked together on the management level. In about half the cases in my sample, that volume doubled at the very least! I know why it happened in the case of the Syms family business: My father and I bring out the best in each other. As Sy says, "We egg each other on."

And there were other surprises:

1. *Considering that there is a 50 percent divorce rate in this country, I found that my respondents worked very hard on their marriages. They really wanted them to last.*

Richard and Judy Joyce of Sherwood, Oregon, third-generation fruit tree and nursery stock growers, who were survivors of farming's Terrible Eighties, agree. "If we had divorced," remembered Richard, "there would have been no way at all of keeping the farm together. Judy was here when we were expanding and buying property, and she was entitled to her share."

And Susan Traub, who works in her father's publishing business, thought it was actually easier to handle a marriage in a family business, "because the business will give you the extra time you need and the understanding if there's a problem."

According to many of the family business members that I spoke with, good marriages make life in the company that much easier, and bad marriages can lead to ghastly and distracting complications. "The marriage is the bedrock of the family business," *Black Enterprise* publisher Earl Graves tells each of his sons. "Think carefully about how this is your partner for life. The marriage will keep your mind free for business if it's good, and will interfere with everything if it's bad."

2. *If the founder is a father, mothers usually have no place in the business.* Not officially, with a title and a salary. Only two second-generation businesses in my survey could be called "mom-and-pop" operations. In *all* the others, mothers played

the traditional role of mediator, child raiser, and soother of troubled waters. Their lack of real power in the family firm compelled many of them into community and philanthropic activities and, in a few instances, into businesses of their own.

3. *In-laws usually are not welcome.* No issue raises more dissent than whether spouses of family members should be allowed to work in the family firm. In my survey, seven families actually forbade the inclusion of in-laws. The others said that there was no absolute rule against such hiring. Only one son-in-law had been made heir apparent.

4. *The Law of Primogeniture is alive and well in the family business.*

Of the heads of family businesses who were founders or who succeeded to the throne, about half were firstborn or only children, accounting for the high number of entrepreneurs who go into business for themselves precisely because they're *not* firstborn. And of the second-generation heirs apparent, almost all were firstborn or only children. Every female head of a company was firstborn like myself, with the exception of two women whose older brothers did not want to go into the family business, bequeathing the mantle to them by default.

5. *There is an absence of nonfamily partners beyond the founding generation.*

The one family in my study in which the business cannot be passed on to the second generation is also the one family in which there is a nonfamily partner. In most cases, by the second generation the nonfamily participants are bought out, as are uncles, aunts, and cousins, even in the third generation.

(I was interested to learn that the word "nepotism" derives from "nepot," the Latin word for nephew. I wonder if family businesses that avoid branching out in all directions have a better chance of surviving. The almost total absence of many collateral relatives in my sampling of successful businesses seems to indicate that they might.

(I got a great quote and a good laugh from Sam LeFrak, chairman of the Lefrak Organization, the mammoth construction and real estate corporation. Sam LeFrak echoed John F. Kennedy's remark about his brother Robert when he told me, "Nepotism is fine as long as you keep it in the family.")

6. *The best family businesses have an estate plan.*

An independent survey found that only 45 percent of family businesses provide for succession. In my sampling, about 75 percent had estate planning, either in place or in the works. In all cases, it was a hotly discussed topic.

7. *My sample pretty much rejected the idea that business and family life could, and should, be kept separate.*

When asked if they could divorce their business from their family life, the vast majority said, "We don't even try." Family business experts give a lot of advice on how to wear two hats, but the word from the front is to cross that idea off your list as a difficult, if not impossible, task to accomplish.

There were two additional themes brought up by most of my interviewees, both of which are considered conventional family business wisdom by experts in the field. In this case, my group, speaking from firsthand experience, endorsed the experts enthusiastically.

8. *Vital: If you're thinking of entering the family business, go to work somewhere else first.*

In my sample, twenty-four second-generation children got experience elsewhere before coming into the family business. Fifteen joined at their first opportunity after school, and four of those wished they hadn't. The general feeling is that it is very important to try out your skills in unknown territory and get some lumps from someone other than Mom or Dad. As I know from experience, the benefit in self-confidence and independent perspective is irreplaceable.

9. *Also very important—develop a relationship with at least one outside adviser who is not a member of your family.*

You need an outsider's perspective. You could appoint outside board members, outside advisers of all kinds, mentors to help the upcoming generation. When I was learning the business, I had, in addition to my father—who, although not the most patient teacher, was my primary guide—a mentor from outside the business who was very helpful. The most important criterion is that they be experienced—other CEOs are perfect—and that there be no conflict of interest. That means your accountant and lawyer are not eligible.

The above observations and suggestions arose again and again as I talked with my interviewees. They are the truths about successful family businesses. I found that while no two experiences were exactly alike, mostly because of meaningful generational and gender-related differences, each of us was peering at the world from the inside of structures that had a lot in common.

I hope that I have managed to give you an introductory peek into the world of the family business. I will try in coming chapters to fill in the details so that your questions will be answered . . . and your picture complete.

2

What's the Role
of the Family
in Family Business?

One thing is certain about the members of that ultimate family business, Windsor, Inc., the British royal family. They all know what they're going to be doing when they grow up. But for most of the rest of us with a lifelong connection to a family based firm, the path to our involvement with the company is less clearly marked. When our personalities are still embryonic and our talents undeveloped, some of us may think we know what we will want later on in life, but in fact, these early interests are often fantasies, and have to be revised.

And it's not only what *we* might want. The members of the parental generation, our prospective employers, have ideas, too. They might think having a child in the business is a dream come true; or the worst idea since Coke tried to change its formula; or decide to adopt a wait-and-see approach. It all depends on each person's previous life experience. Is the parent the more or less contented son of the company's founder, fulfilling his job as president and working well with his CEO father? Or is she the ambitious daughter of a founder-father who is allowing his children to slug it out for the top managerial job?

I don't think that any of my interviewees would disagree that each family's history is special, and as a result, each has developed family and business interactions that are unique—customized, in a sense.

But I also don't think that any of the family business members to whom I spoke would argue with that much-repeated quotation from Leo Tolstoy's *Anna Karenina:* "Happy families are all alike; every unhappy family is unhappy in its own way."

All functioning families learn to put the greater good above their own narrower self-interest. They learn to trust each other, to communicate, to compromise. When it comes to business, if they do not, then the business is usually sold to outsiders, or fails.

During my interviews, I stuck to my original concept: I was really interested only in those family businesses that not only were doing well financially but also whose members were reasonably satisfied with their lot.

With these criteria in mind, and with the understanding that I was talking with people in different industries, from disparate cultural backgrounds and regions of the country, I still was not surprised to hear many similar childhood experiences described. In general, early recollections were mostly pleasant and positive.

Most of the founder/entrepreneurs that my respondents talked about had forceful, sometimes egocentric, personalities. They knew what was right, and the family had better toe the line. On the other hand, they tried not to smother their children. It's not hard to figure out that if you raise a bunch of indecisive wimps, you're not going to have a child who is one day capable of running your company.

A typical sort of comment comes from Steve Forbes, son of the late Malcolm Forbes, who was a severe disciplinarian and certainly not an easy parent. Steve talked about his father in *Family Business* magazine. Steve remembered that his father "wouldn't tell us to be home at a certain time when we wanted to stay out late, or be up waiting. He figured there were some things that should develop in our personalities without his interference. He certainly wanted a tight grip on things, but he knew when to back off."

Malcolm apparently didn't just play it by ear when raising his children. Even if he found it hard to let go, on some level he wanted independent kids who could fend for themselves.

Each Family's System Has a Life of Its Own
There's a quotation by the Dutch philosopher Baruch Spinoza that I keep in my office for inspiration: "To be what we are and to become what we are capable of becoming is the only end to life." Taken out of context, it could seem a little hokey—the sort of epigraph that might appear at the beginning of a new diet book.

But to me, as a working member of a family business and a functioning member of that family, those words have profound meaning. I see much of my personal development as a seamless continuum from my early days to now. My experience began when I was a young girl—not yet thirteen—running the cash register in one of my father's stores in downtown New York City or learning how to arrange stock during various summer jobs. So have other children of entrepreneurs done for centuries.

I know that even among the people I have met who are successfully involved with family businesses there are stories of childhood experiences far from the norm of the "happy family." But my search was for patterns of behavior that work. In childhood, did my now grown-up respondents feel connected to a larger group? Were they given an opportunity to explore, to learn independence and leadership, to develop creativity in order to start on the path to adult development espoused by Spinoza?

During the 1960s a new field of psychotherapy became popular —that of family therapy. Murray Bowen, a psychiatrist working with schizophrenics, gradually came to the conclusion that the only way truly to understand the patient was to see that person in the context of his or her own family.

Bowen had found that even if a schizophrenic patient made progress in an institutional setting, when the patient was returned to the family, schizophrenic behavior patterns returned. Clearly, this must have something to do with the effect of family dynamics on the patient. Bowen came to see the patient as a component of a family system, and not someone who developed the behavior patterns on his or her own or who could be treated in a vacuum. This was seminal thinking for the time, and his ideas were quickly adopted by others in the field of individual counseling.

Dr. Michael E. Kerr, writing in *Handbook of Family Therapy,* said of Bowen: "Bowen was beginning to find it impossible to see a single person without automatically 'seeing' the entire family like phantoms alongside. This growing perception of one person as a segment of the larger family system had come to govern the way he thought about and responded to the individual. Psychoanalytic interpretations of behavior were giving way to seeing the *functional significance* of that behavior in relationship to the family system. No longer was the family seen as a collection of individuals, each operating out of his or her own unconscious conflicts. Now the functioning of each member was seen as integrally tied to that of every other member."

Of course, a lot of adult members of family businesses spend thousands of dollars on their own psychotherapy to achieve what they perceive as necessary separation from their parents and other kin, but it is undeniably true that we all are the way we are at least partially because of family influences stemming back to our earliest days. If we are going to join in an office situation those who had such a powerful influence on us when we were young, we had better make sure that we've moved beyond childhood dynamics— and the only way that we can do that is to understand them.

One of the wonderful things about life is that we can change. We can gain confidence, improve our appearance, learn more effective business techniques, work on our personal relationships. We come to adult life with our own ideas, interests, and reactions —not all of them admirable. These traits develop over the years, starting very early on, and depend on our own family's dynamics. In a sense, whatever our family's system was, and is, it's ours, too. On a positive note, when we reach the age of analysis, we can perhaps, with the help of others, change lifelong patterns that are not in our own self-interest and that might not contribute to the greater good.

The Family as an American Institution
In researching this book, I did not really expect sexy revelations about why family businesses work. I think, in fact, I was expecting what I did get—rather homely repetitions of truths that I suspected existed, but wanted verified. Families that succeed practice many of the "traditional" virtues: loyalty and trust, sharing of goals, belief in the importance of the family, mutual appreciation of each other, a sense of collective mastery of their own destiny, and the ability to deal with crises in a constructive way—all important components of effective communication.

When these traits are practiced conscientiously by the group, whether in a family or a family business setting, they usually spell success.

O. M. "Koke" Cummins, president of Mansfield Industries, an Ohio-based metallurgical corporation, echoed the observations of many interviewees when, in describing his durable marriage, he mused: "I wonder if they don't go hand-in-hand more frequently than we realize—success in family business and success in the family setting? I wonder if the kinds of traits that bring success in one setting also don't bring success in the other?"

I agree. Family businesses are not run by Jekylls-and-Hydes. If thoughtful relationships are the norm at home, and family members take it as a given that they are to behave in a civilized manner, then these good manners will usually extend to interactions in the workplace. A woman who has always looked up to a much-loved older brother is unlikely to turn on him unexpectedly in a board meeting. Successful families that are in business together enjoy the ties that bind.

"FAMILY" AND "BUSINESS"—A DIFFICULT COMBINATION

There is no easy definition of "family" because family structure is viewed differently depending on who it is who's doing the looking. A psychologist will concentrate on family relationships; a sociologist, the family's place in the community; an economist, its place in the commercial life of a country. When we talk about a family business, all these points of view must apply, because when the kids join their parents in the workplace, the resulting mix is going to have at least minimal effect on every aspect of all their lives. Suddenly, that long weekend is not possible because Dad needs you at a meeting on Monday morning. Or you have to negotiate with your child because it's time for his or her annual salary review —a very different business from setting an appropriate allowance in high school. And what if you have holiday plans that don't involve your family? Will your folks be offended and will this irritation pop up at the office? All these problems arose in the lives of my respondents, along with others—they're built into family business dynamics.

Some family business analysts point out that the perfect arrangement is to treat your job in the family business like any other. You are a professional, and you will treat your relatives like other professionals no matter what the realities of the situation. Easy to say, hard to do, especially when bickering is the natural form of conversation in your family.

But reality notwithstanding, you can continue to strive for better relationships—there are communications techniques that can be applied in an attempt at distance and privacy. You also have to accept a big slice of reality, as described by G. Jeff Mennen, who was, until recently, vice chairman of the Mennen Company, a fourth-generation personal products manufacturer that has been acquired by the Colgate-Palmolive Company. Laughing when I asked him how he managed to separate his business from his personal life, Mennen said, "There's no question that you cannot separate your business from your family life if you're in a family owned company. It's the rock around which everybody gathers."

Mennen also touched on the ambiguity that we talked about in the previous chapter, the basic incompatibility of "family" and "business." The two elements are not a happy couple, and, like in a marriage, one has to develop techniques to manage intrinsic conflict. This processing of conflict becomes fundamental to the smooth management of any family business, and underlies the happiness of family members who work there.

"The family is basically a supportive and nurturing group," Mennen pointed out, "whereas business is concerned with performance only. As in, What did you do for me today? Those two are in conflict, and it's only when you are in a family that owns a business that you bring both of them together constantly. If you're working for General Motors, for example, and you have a bad day at the office—somehow you design the fenders wrong on the car —you can go home, put it all behind you, and have people who will say, 'Don't worry about it. Things will be better tomorrow.' You can start to feel good again. In a family owned business, you're with the company twenty-four hours a day."

All of us who work within a family business have to deal with this paradox of the sometimes antithetical goals of family and business all the time, with varying degrees of success. My results-oriented father does not have too much difficulty these days in treating me as a business associate. But others of my interviewees have more trouble achieving adult status in the eyes of Mom or Pop. Whatever our individual situations, we are all involved heavily with our families, and all are a result of our life experiences within those families.

The Family Dance

Since it is true that families and businesses of all sorts, including family businesses, are variations on a structural theme, experiences within the family individually govern what sort of person will present himself or herself to the workplace. We certainly can work on perceived faults, but we cannot really invent our own personalities; like it or not, we are largely the product of our early experiences.

Family Business Consultant Kathleen Wiseman refers to the "family dance" in describing the sorts of family interrelationships that everyone develops. Wiseman said: "The family for me is a formalization of relationships that provide connections that are the glue that brings individuals into the systems. It is not a collection of individuals, it is a group that is formed together and responds and reacts and walks through life's experiences together." In other words, these people have a shared family history, shared customs, and shared ways of reacting to life's events.

Wiseman continued: "And these systems have very clear boundaries of who is in, and who is out. A system for me is a way of looking at the world."

The child's way of looking at the world is in large part formed by early experiences within the family. Family patterns are set and in time everyone learns the steps to the family dance. If Sibling A behaves in a certain way, you can pretty much predict the reaction of Sibling B—the dance has been danced a thousand times. How will this affect the business if this particular dance is nonproductive and is still being performed during the workday by competing siblings?

Roles within a family are assigned early, frequently having to do with birth order. It's no accident that most of the company presidents that I met during my interviewing were firstborn. Growing up, they get a lot of attention, and suffer under a lot of pressure. They are expected to succeed, to take charge, and they, in fact, often do. With this sort of reputation, firstborns are usually welcomed enthusiastically into a family business, but what if you are the middle child? Traditionally, these children might be overlooked within the family and may not develop strong leadership skills while young. What happens when they try to make a place for themselves in the family business? Are they taken seriously? Maybe not.

All of this can be overcome, of course, with ambition and hard work and a little luck, but I have found that all those images of a child as the "pretty one," or the "smart one," or the "funny one" —stereotypes that may, in fact, be long outgrown—have a tendency to stick long after the child is an adult and has developed a multifaceted personality, elements of which may be completely overlooked by family members who see them only in one well-known dimension.

The second characteristic isolated by Kathleen Wiseman that affects adult behavior is the importance of family history.

What happens when there is negative family history? How many of us in family businesses are still suffering for slights committed a generation ago? Not all, it's true, but I have to go no farther than my own family's history for a good example. My father did very well financially after leaving his brother's employment in the late 1950s, but the rift that led to his departure was never repaired. The result was a lifetime of awkwardness for all the relatives involved.

One basic truth that I have learned during this project is that it's *always* better not to have irrevocable disagreements with siblings. The resulting stress, as well as strain on family loyalties, is excruciating. I know from my own experience with my brothers that if we knew in advance how much pain can be caused by family upheaval, we would try whatever arbitration open to us to avoid it.

The foundation for sibling rivalry is, of course, laid in childhood, and I can see now that it's important to establish patterns of compromise, shared values, and a sense of right and wrong from the very start.

Family business consultant Barbara Hollander, after years of observing every conceivable kind of problem that could arise in a family run company, thinks that serious, win-at-all-costs sibling competitiveness, at any age, "can never really be productive. I call that kind of competitiveness the 'lollipop syndrome,' in which people are still counting how many yellows you have, and how many greens. Intrafamily competition in a family business *must* be balanced with respect for collaboration. I can think of one family that works well together who sometimes see tensions building up." Their solution: " 'We two brothers will go into a closet and hammer it out and we'll come out and we'll be okay.' "

This story has to do with siblings, but the same rules apply to interaction between parents and children, or to any family relationship. Goodwill and compromise really can help overcome real problems; without them, it is most likely that the structure of both the family and the business will splinter apart.

So while family history can be negative, with all sorts of residual problems and resentments still hanging around the various generations, there also is positive family history. When it exists, all generations pull together to keep the business running smoothly. Family histories go through cycles as the new generations are born, grow up, and become adults. In time, the older family members die, and the children move up a level to take their place. Earlier in this chapter we talked about the elements that must be present for a family, and a family business, to be successful, among them commitment, loyalty, the ability to communicate, and the wisdom to handle crises.

But if we look at families as an evolving organism, which I think we must, there are two more characteristics that are basic to business success and that come into play as the children grow up.

The first involves the question of expectations being met and fulfilled and early exposure to the family business. A surprisingly large percentage of my interviewees said that they were not urged, in so many words, to come into the business. And most of the entrepreneurial generation, when I asked them if they had pressured their children to join them, said that they had not—the choice was that of the child.

But many members of the second generation, while protesting that it was their idea to join their parents in the business, admitted to having had heavy-duty influences that were "just around" during their childhood years. The word used most often was "osmosis": as in, "I guess when you're around something a great deal you learn a lot by osmosis," said Kathryn Klinger, president of the cosmetics and skin-care company founded by her mother, Georgette Klinger. "My mother would discuss the business at home and after school I would bring my homework and I would sit and do it in her office. And she'd be on the phone or she'd be telling something to one of the staff, and I'd see a lot and hear a lot. It was just so much a part of life that I was learning without realizing I was learning."

This is almost automatic apprenticeship, and if the child learns through the pores of his or her skin, in a reasonably nonstressful way, is it any wonder that the family business seems an attractive choice when the child reaches the age of choosing an occupation?

The second element that I think must be present within the family as the children mature is adaptability, the ability to change, to learn new things. Family business consultant David Bork, in talking about "being able to operate effectively as a family and within the family business enterprise," said his researchers have "discovered that it's an important thing for families to learn together."

It's vital not only to learn new things, but also to learn how to change. If companies don't change, they will die. It's been that way ever since the dawn of civilization, when ambitious entrepreneurs tried to figure out what their customers wanted and how to get it to them. We figured out about shipping silk and tea a long time ago, but new challenges arise every day because economic certainties never are certain.

I should also mention a trait that is essential—especially for the upcoming generation—in the smooth relationships among and between generations. Leonard Lauder, who is chief executive officer of the cosmetics company founded by his mother, Estee Lauder, and his father, Joseph, told the readers of *Family Business* magazine recently that "patience is the key" in working within a family business. Certainly that has been key in my case: I know that change comes slowly, and I try to build my case carefully before approaching my father with a suggestion.

In trying to isolate the most important characteristics that are present in successful families, it seems clear that almost every trait has something to do with adaptability. Families that work have the ability to sit down together and discuss a problem dispassionately. They are willing to try something new if the old system is outdated. And if true adaptability and the ability to change exist, family members may have a real chance to prove themselves in new roles, and put to rest forever those awful childhood stereotypes that haunt most of us.

I Learn to Persevere

If what we become is in large part a result of our childhood, what lessons did I learn from mine?

Independence, I think, and an ability to make my own way along a path that *I* chose, despite discouragement. In addition, I must have absorbed a strong family feeling and great admiration for my father, because when the time came for me to make a commitment to his company, I did so willingly . . . if anxiously.

Because I am the oldest of Sy Syms' six children, I am the one who remembers what it was like when he was a struggling entrepreneur. Our household during those early days was a traditional one. It was always assumed that my three brothers would join the business and that I would be a "teacher, or something like that." At least, that's what my mother thought. Her logic was straightforward: "A grade school teacher can be home in time to take care of her husband and children." I don't remember being especially upset by this judgment. When I was very young, I probably thought that's what girls ought to do. I certainly changed my mind very early on, but like most women of my generation, that early relegating of us to second-class status economically took an unconscious toll in self-esteem and ambition.

My earliest conscious memories start around my fourth birthday, when my family at the time—my parents, brother Stephen, and I—moved from the Flatbush area of Brooklyn and our one-bedroom apartment to a house that seemed a mansion to me in Yonkers, a suburb just north of Manhattan.

Soon after we moved, my mother gave birth to another brother, Robert. At two-year intervals the family grew to include Richard, Laura, and finally the youngest, Adrienne. What had seemed unbelievably grand to me became a little house with eight people and one bathroom. My father was the first up in the morning, then my mother, and I was usually next, and so on down the line until all eight of us were launched into the world for another day.

Our neighborhood, Lincoln Park, had a great many first-generation Americans like my father and mother, all upwardly mobile, all of whom believed in the American promise of a better life.

I loved living in Yonkers. I loved the ethnic mix. My father and mother held very liberal beliefs, which sounded right to me. My father would tell us that no matter how different people might look, we were all basically alike: "When people bleed, they all have the same color blood," he said. His idols were Adlai Stevenson and Eleanor Roosevelt and I bought into his progressive attitudes enthusiastically. Before second grade, my best friends in the neighborhood were John Salltrees, who was Jamaican, and Addie Denatelli, a Roman Catholic Italian-American. Life was rich and interesting.

By 1965, the years of penny-pinching and sacrifice were to be rewarded. We were going to move, my parents announced to us one day, to a Georgian Colonial house in Bronxville where we could each have our own bedroom!

Everything changed when we moved to nearby Bronxville. By that time, I was a sophomore in high school, and the business that Dad had started when I was nine had begun to be successful.

At first I felt like a princess in a fairy tale. I loved our new house. But my enthusiasm turned into despair within just a few days of starting at my new school. That wonderful ethnic mix was something that we had apparently left behind forever when we left Yonkers. I had never seen so many tall, blond, blue-eyed teens in my life. Their world seemed unfamiliar to me, and we just didn't seem to *get* each other. It wasn't long before I realized that I was the only Jewish girl in Bronxville High.

My first year was awful. There were six or seven senior boys who were especially cruel—their teasing frightened me. And although I did have a lot of girlfriends, I was invisible to the male population.

I tried not to let my social status as pariah ruin my life. I lost weight, straightened my hair every morning with an iron, and tried out for the cheerleading squad. I became active on campus. I was a member of the student government, president of the chorus, advertising manager of the school newspaper, and, after appearing in several school plays, had gained a reputation as a talented actress.

I had been a pretty good student in Yonkers, but I found the kids in Bronxville to be at least a year ahead of me scholastically. In addition to my various activities, I had to study three or four hours a night to keep up.

I actually made the cheerleading squad, but it didn't help—my untouchable status remained. In the three years that I spent at that high school, I had only one date with a Bronxville boy. I really did feel like an outcast and I lived for the summers. As a counselor at a camp far from Bronxville, I never failed to cultivate a boyfriend.

Some of my siblings were having tough times, too. The younger kids—Richard, Laura, and Adrienne—were cute and fair and had an easier time. But Stephen and Robert were as miserable as I was. More than once they had come home with black eyes, covered with bruises. I later found out that when some of our neighbors found out that we were Jewish, a petition was circulated in an attempt to prevent our moving in.

For months I complained to my parents, with ever-increasing desperation. My parents listened attentively but they had little choice since the cost of replacing that spacious house, purchased at a fire sale, would have been more than we could afford.

But those fourteen rooms had completely lost their magic for me. I didn't care if I had my own bathroom—there were no parties for me to get dressed up for. Reluctantly, I agreed to give the place one more year. If things hadn't improved by then, my parents promised, they would give in and we would move.

But when the time came, my father had to renege on his promise, breaking my heart. "Marcy," he said sympathetically, "you just have to learn to treat school as if it were a job." I'm sure that's what he believed at the time, but by the time I had graduated, each of my siblings had been sent to a school outside the Bronxville system.

As I look back, I don't remember those years with much pleasure, but from my current vantage, I can appreciate the experience. I learned how not to be a quitter, and I learned how to tolerate not being popular, and I learned to deal with disappointment.

But for years I could find no silver lining in this unhappy period of my life until an older friend, upon hearing my tale of woe, said: "Aren't you lucky? You learned early how to handle disappointment. Some people don't learn it in their lifetime." And another insightful friend told me: "You ought to thank those people for teaching you about prejudice early. Life is easier with fewer surprises."

They were right. And I have tried to extract from the legacy of my childhood the ability to think positively—to win *something* positive from every experience, whether trying or joyous.

Each family is special—and so, by extension, is each family business. "I think of a family as having its own DNA," said Kathleen Wiseman. "And one of the things that make family business difficult is that the family patterns, structures, and messages get taken into the business." These are the patterns that are internalized during childhood, and that will continue through adolescence and into adulthood. If they work for the company, and are satisfying to the individual, then we can expect that person to become a useful member of the family business.

I think we can make a case for the DNA analogy. After all, each family is a unique organism, made up of equally unique elements —its members. My growing-up years were not wholly pleasant, it's true, but they were mine alone. It's results that count and, remembering Spinoza's urging to become the best that we can be, one can view life as a continuum along which we all can learn and improve.

I believe that you really do learn through adversity. I don't regret my childhood. Not every child has to live with disappointment, or experience the pain in being an outsider. But I was stubborn, and I persevered. I *wanted* to be happy, and frequently was. Today, I know that happiness is only momentary and that we must strive for contentment, which can be achieved by arranging our lives in a way that is satisfying and morally consistent with our belief. I think, at least for me, it's also vital to make morally correct decisions.

I think that those difficult early times made me better able to deal with the worries and disasters that I have encountered as an adult. I know that an unfortunate situation can improve, and also that it's within my power to make it better. The important thing is that I make decisions I can live with and be proud of, regardless of the situation.

The best things that a well-ordered family can teach you are self-reliance, self-respect, and self-esteem. If you understand these three traits, and can number them among your own, then you can probably handle anything that life dishes out, and your family training can be considered a success.

Chapter

3

The Family Name
and All That
It Incorporates

One of the characteristics of a family business that separates it from a company that is not family run is its history. Everyone involved knows how, when, and by whom the business started. Family members also know why the company is called what it's called—frequently the family name is involved—and how the company has changed since its original conception. And, most importantly, this knowledge is meaningful to the family member. It may be part of his or her self-image and feeling of identification with the family group.

But there's a lot more to it than a simple recounting of chronology. There should be no confusion about the importance of family tradition, and the value of using the family name. The history that I've discussed above may have several elements: it's a story of how things started, it may set the stage for traditions that are passed from one generation to the next, and, although starting as a simple story, it may become larger than life and achieve a mythic quality. By the time you travel from story to myth, the myth has taken on a symbolic meaning, which transcends the ordinary facts of the story.

MYTHS AND FAMILY TRADITION

If myths are symbolic stories that explain something—a social custom, some aspect of a religion, the birth of a nation—then it's clear that every institution will have a body of myth appropriate to its history. Families, too, include them in their body of oral tradition. They're the stories that are told when families get together on the occasions that enhance family identity.

Business consultant Barbara Hollander talked with me about the importance of tradition within a family business: "It's a commitment to the tradition and the history and the values of the family, as well as a sense of obligation" that lies at the core of a successful family business. "This isn't a negative obligation on the part of the third, fourth, or fifth generation," she continued. "But rather, a desire to carry on. This is a very strong motivator. Nobody wants to be the one who went down with the ship."

Every family has traditions that set them apart from all other families, but there seems to be a correlation between the importance of tradition and family business success—more is definitely better. Family business expert David Bork has noted that out of the 250 families he has worked with since 1970, about 25 percent were Jewish, a much higher percentage than their share of the general population: "In the Jewish religion there are more traditions than in all the gentile families," he theorized. For example, at the Passover seder, worldwide, the youngest child in a Jewish family will ask, "Why is this night different from any other night?" No matter the family, the answer is always the same, as the story familiar to all Jews is told and retold every year.

Thus, members of the Jewish religion, like observers of other fully developed faiths with belief systems that govern a large part of daily custom, grow up comfortable with the presence of influential traditions, whether in religion or family life.

Each family moves through time creating its own history, and, like a fingerprint, it is different from all others. Each family builds around that history a code, most likely unspoken, that every family member knows, seemingly from birth.

In the Syms family, there are rules for being a Syms, which are somehow understood by all family members, whether or not they are followed to the letter.

Bork, during a recent lecture at his institute in Aspen, Colorado, pointed out that the significance of tradition is not wholly understood, but its power is unmistakable.

"The Bork family eats cranberry sauce on top of its pumpkin pie," he told his audience. "I grew up watching my father do it. You may crinkle your lips at such an extraordinary combination (which I admit is a little tart), but the point is, when the family had a gathering down in Georgia recently, I arranged for the dessert to be cranberry sauce on pumpkin pie. We sat around the table and ate it and told stories about my father, and pretty soon, there wasn't a dry eye in the place."

Another moving example of intentional family bonding is an odyssey enjoyed each Labor Day by the Woods family, of New York City's Sylvia's Restaurant. The family travels to South Carolina, to their original hometown, to meet with relatives from all over the country. Their Labor Day tradition fills a need unique to many African American families originally from the South. The Woods family annual trip has become a meaningful new tradition —it combines some of a new way of life with the history of the generations that came before.

And whenever families gather, they tell stories. Over time, the stories become traditional, and then become mythic symbols of that family's tradition. Whether the myths that support traditions are true, or pure fabrication, they give validity, life, a sense of purpose, and group identity to the people associated with whatever history is being recounted. Throughout time, humankind seems to need and want these myths because they help to explain the meaning of our lives. They speak from beyond the grave and give us reasons for perpetuating tradition.

My Dad, the Hero

Family business stories—the kind that have been retold forever and give a special aura to the actors and episodes involved— should begin with "Once upon a time . . ." because they all do eventually acquire a mythic patina. After the hundredth retelling, every person and event is much larger than life, and all the rough edges of the story have been smoothed away.

One Syms family myth is a David-and-Goliath story starring my dad, Sy. The plot shows him upholding the rights of the small businessman against New York City's mega-developers. No one works around Sy for long without hearing how, in the late 1960s, a small off-price menswear retail store owner in Lower Manhattan fended off U.S. Steel, no less, which was trying to erect a fifty-story office building on a site that was home to one of Sy's stores.

A headline in *The Wall Street Journal* of September 18, 1967, provides black-and-white documentation: "A Small Haberdashery Upsets U.S. Steel's Skyscraper Project." That's my dad.

It seems that Sy had a lease that ran for thirty days, and he didn't want to move until then. Business was booming despite the presence of scaffolding and heavy building equipment. The $22,000 settlement offered was inadequate. Unless U.S. Steel made it worth his while, he would stay put. The result: Sy prevailed and became a real estate legend.

To me, my father is both a hero and a practical man. He not only leads us, he delivers in a way that means money in the bank. The myth clearly defines him. By knowing his story, you understand who Sy is, as well as learning something of his toughness and his principles. It relates to our competitiveness as a company. It says to us today that even though we're not as old an off-price company as Loehmann's, or as big an off-price company as Burlington Coat Factory, we are tough and stubborn and agile. It also says that if there were to be a shakeout of off-price retailers, we would survive and prosper.

Additionally, the meaning of the myth relates to our own management style and corporate culture, which respects the contributions one individual can make to alter the future of the whole.

My family story is not about size or strength but of courage, stamina, and moral influence. My father is not really larger than life. He's a familiar figure on a television screen whose philosophy is simple: respect for the customer. He tells people about his stores without carrying on. And when he's told you what he thinks you need to know, he shuts up. When explaining how he likes to do business Sy typically might say: "Don't put me on and don't complicate this thing. It's just a sweater. Tell me it's 100 percent cotton or whatever, but don't tell me what it was, or what it's going to be. Just give the one price and let me go."

THE CONCEPT OF "OFF PRICE" BUYING AND SELLING

Part of my father's tradition that has become the foundation of our company culture involves his simplicity, authenticity, and directness. Sy trusts his customers to make up their own minds about what they want. Adhering to his principle of respect for the customer, my father expanded his company twelvefold in ten years. From his first venture in 1959 until this writing, Sy has transformed his holdings from one little store in downtown New York City to twenty-nine stores, approximately 1 million square feet of selling space, around the country.

Historically, Dad's business did well, but not spectacularly well until the mid-1960s. Then he had the first of a series of very good ideas, each of which paid off. With every success, the Sy Syms myth grew.

The first good idea involved the concept of "off price" buying and selling: buying for less than wholesale and selling for less than normal retail.

In 1959, when Syms first opened, consumerism was being invented. New laws required that labels on merchandise be honest and complete. Irregulars had to be clearly marked so consumers would know what they were buying. In this new atmosphere, Sy Syms opened a store that bought brand-name irregulars for less than wholesale and sold them for less than normal retail because they were irregulars. Then and now, buying for less than wholesale was the guiding principle. It was defined as "off price." Everyone benefited—manufacturers disposed of troublesome irregulars and consumers had the option of buying imperfect merchandise for less.

Today, irregulars are a small part of our business, primarily because, as time passed, another burden on manufacturers became an off-price opportunity. Manufacturers never sold out to the last piece. If someone was willing and able to buy these leftovers, manufacturers found it worthwhile to sell them for less. Syms was willing and able. Our objective was to pay manufacturers their cost. By selling to us at cost, manufacturers could dispose of their overproduction and stabilize their profits. Their businesses could grow, and some of the guesswork was eliminated from their sales projections.

At Syms today, we are aware that we are different from other retail categories. We cannot imitate. We cannot compromise for short-term objectives. Our principles define us.

We must:

- Buy brand names at, or close to, a manufacturer's cost.
- Create and maintain mutually profitable relationships with brand-name manufacturers.
- Sell to consumers in a no-frills atmosphere at prices 40 to 70 percent below normal retail.
- Avoid fashion decisions, but offer the widest selection possible of brands, sizes, styles, and colors.
- Merchandise our stores logically to make it easy for consumers to shop.

At Syms, we don't deviate from these principles. Our success today is based solely on how well we execute them.

A Few More Good Ideas
When Sy Syms decided to take a chance on off-price retailing, time proved him right. Within eight years, he was able to buy out his partner. Sy was ready to expand with the help of a loyal stable of vendors who were sure he would live up to his promise never to use their names in advertising.

In the beginning, Syms followed early discounting tradition by removing labels from the clothing. Even today, although manufacturers' labels remain, the brand names are not used in our national advertising. Faithful Syms customers know that they will find recognizable brand names at 40 to 70 percent off regular department store prices when they come into the store.

Instead of feeling threatened by the consumer movement of the seventies, my father capitalized on it. He had always given customers respect, assuming every person who walked into his store was at least as intelligent as he and worked as hard for his or her money. Sy built his business on the premise that if consumers knew as much about clothing as he did, they would always check out Syms first, even if we couldn't satisfy their needs on every visit.

As sales increased, my father had the confidence to open several small stores close to the original one. But with each of the four openings, he noticed that the all-important efficiency factor went down. He just didn't have time any longer to talk with each customer who came into the store as he used to do. Sy would always say something like, "When I opened my second store, I decreased my company's efficiency by 50 percent because I couldn't be in two stores at the same time."

My father says he stumbled on the solution to his problem by accident: "In 1971, our accountants told us it was foolish not to advertise because we were going to have to pay taxes anyway if we didn't. I had never spent a dime on advertising. It was all word-of-mouth."

But Sy decided to heed the accountants' advice. He chose radio advertising and jumped in with both feet. He did everything: writing the scripts and then reading them, in the matter-of-fact, straightforward manner of the professional sportscaster he had been in the late 1940s.

Financial necessity had forced Sy to leave sportscasting to try his hand at retailing, which he hoped would provide a steadier, better-paid job alternative. Now the descriptive style of the sportscaster, the directness of the man, and the focus on a unique retail operation made the commercials effective.

With the radio commercials bringing in a steady stream of customers to his stores, Sy not only expanded each year, but achieved his second objective. His presence was now felt throughout his company thanks to his advertising, even though he couldn't be in two places at once.

In April of 1973, Sam DeLucca, a former New York Jets All-Star offensive lineman who later became a broadcaster and was a regular customer, came in to shop. DeLucca bought a couple of suits and then asked Sy for a gift certificate to be given on the air to a football star during a pregame television show on NBC. In exchange, Sy would get air time to advertise his stores.

When we children gathered around the TV set that Sunday we were all terribly impressed. Sy, who was doing his own ad, as he did on radio, was just like Sy at home—no gimmicks, no phoniness, just down-to-earth, direct, and sincere.

That first TV ad in 1974 was a sixty-second spot in which Sy laid out his advertising concepts for the next decade. He explained off-price, keystoning (doubling) the "wholesale price," the importance of brand labels, and why he would never run a sale. With his respect for the consumer, he gave them the information and left it up to them to use it.

And he knew what he was doing. "When I first started advertising the store on television," he explained, "I assumed a lot of viewers thought I was an actor who happened to look like a merchant. It took several years before the public started to believe there really was a guy named Sy Syms and that he worked in the store."

And if customers began to know what he looked like, so did his employees. He finally had achieved that important omnipresence. In the stores, Sy jokingly referred to his TV image as "Big Brother" looking over everyone.

Important words often become part of the family myth. In 1974, Sy came up with his slogan, "An educated consumer is our best customer," probably the best-known retailing phrase since the Good Housekeeping Seal of Approval. Sy had plenty of good customers, and during the next decade they flocked to Syms.

Through all the years of expansion, my father has remained the same. You can't seem real in front of the camera unless you are. As the stories tell, my father found a way to market his good ideas. You can have one really good idea a day, but if you don't catch the consumer's attention, and in a big way, nobody will know.

THE POWER OF THE FAMILY NAME

If a family's myth gives meaning to its history, both within and without the business, the family name is the symbol of everything for which the family business stands.

As a trademark, the name is protected by business owners as if it were its most precious tangible asset—which it may well be. Part of the strength of the family name is derived from the fact that, unlike such corporate names as Exxon, which are chosen for their lack of meaning in English, the family name is attached to real people and their history.

G. Jeff Mennen, former vice chairman of the Mennen Company, commented on this important difference between family and corporate names: "There's a tendency in publicly owned companies to deal with the firm as an inanimate thing, whereas in a family business you are a living part of the community. I read in *Family Business Magazine* that the *Valdez* oil spill in Alaska caused by a giant corporation was cleaned up by a small family business—petroleum pick-up experts Dave Usher, his son, son-in-law, and godson."

The power of the family name is not just an abstract entity. In fact, its value has been measured and found to give businesses a creative edge and even increase its chances for survival. According to a 1989 survey of 1,076 family businesses conducted by *Family Business* magazine, 48 percent of the families surveyed used their name as the company name. Could their culture be stronger because their name is on the door? Could pride, commitment, and passion be enhanced because of their name identification?

According to the survey, the types of business in which the family name was most likely to be the company name were: construction (75 percent of companies); financial/insurance/real estate (58 percent); wholesale/retail (49 percent), and manufacturing (41 percent).

Of the families whose name was the company name, 20 percent of respondents talked about "respect for the name" as one of its three top business priorities, as opposed to 9 percent for families who did not use their own name. And 59 percent of companies that did use their name concentrated on it in advertising.

There's no escaping the fact that a company's practices will reflect the personal values of the people who are running the shop, no matter what the size. It's been my experience that if your name is the one on the building, you'd better have a clear idea of how that name is perceived by your customers. You can't afford to lose your good name—it's absolutely unthinkable from both a business and personal point of view.

One inspiring example of the power of a good name is Frieda Caplan, founder of Frieda's, Inc. She started her company in 1957 in California, delivering first-rate produce herself in the family station wagon. Since then, her name, synonymous with excellence, has become the signature on the "designer fruit" industry. Today her one-of-a-kind company has sales of $20 million a year.

I asked Caplan whether the use of her name had been an intentional marketing ploy, to make it appear as if a real person was choosing every piece of kiwi that went to market.

Not at all, she told me. Originally, in fact, the name of the company was Produce Specialties, Inc. Then, as the company expanded, they developed new packaging and used the term "Frieda's Finest" for some of their items. That caught on, and clients and customers remembered it and asked for Frieda's produce by name. So, during the seventies, the company officially changed its name to Frieda's Finest/Produce Specialties, Inc.

Frieda said she had to get used to seeing her name on her business's packaging. "I was very uncomfortable with it at first," she said. "I just didn't recognize the marketing value.

"In the beginning," Frieda continued, "before we had established our own sales staff, clients would call and insist on talking to Frieda, instead of just someone at Frieda's who could take an order."

As Frieda's Finest became big business, people assumed that the name was just something that made good public relations. "Now, many people don't even know there's a Frieda. We get letters, because each of our packages has an invitation to write to us for more recipes, and they'll say things like: 'Dear Frieda, if there really is one, or are you another Betty Crocker?'"

To make sure that customers get the message that there really is a Frieda at Frieda's, Inc., a picture of the founder now appears on each package.

Caplan's story of the evolving company name came to an end in January 1990: "Because there was such confusion in the trade—

some would still call us Produce Specialties, Inc., some Frieda's Finest, others the whole thing . . . we took a survey of our clients throughout the country and asked their opinion." The response was overwhelming and settled the question: "They all said to change it to Frieda's, Inc., period. And that's what everyone calls us now."

And what does it mean to have your name on your product? It means a lot, and is tied in with your company's reputation and your personal pride. Said Caplan: "It really forces you to maintain a quality product. Since we might have at any one time at least 250 different products under our label, you know darn well that if somebody picks up something of ours and they're unhappy with it, there are 249 other items that they're not going to buy. You cannot afford to have anything less than the best if it's under your name."

Even when a family name is a real tongue-wrapper, it can be a proven business asset. Bernadette Castro, the president of her family's business, Castro Convertibles, says she encourages young entrepreneurs to put their name on the door: "Unless it's got seven syllables, I don't care what it is. Create a media personality, make a celebrity out of yourself. It's the greatest marketing strategy in the world."

To prove Castro's point, we have the story of Orville Redenbacher. When he first decided to market his quality popcorn, he went to Daniel Edelman, a public relations consultant who, with his son Richard and daughter Renee, was among the people I interviewed. After meeting Redenbacher, Edelman told his client to go with his unusual name. "I could have saved me the $11,000," Redenbacher replied. "My mother told me to do that twenty years ago."

Edelman also told Redenbacher to appear on TV himself to advertise his product—the rest is quality popcorn history.

The Benefits of Family Membership

Within the family, those who have the "name" seem to cherish it. Steve Karol is chief executive officer of HMK, his family's holding company in Waltham, Massachusetts. HMK is a diversified business dealing in steel, transportation, and office furniture that Karol and his two brothers have run since their father died in 1983 at age fifty-five. Karol described how capitalizing on the power of a name is not only necessary but essential for success in a family owned business: "In our family we like to joke that we Karols are an ordained race, but, in fact, I'm not going to let my daughters take anyone else's name. I think their husbands should take *theirs* instead! A family that doesn't have the strength of chauvinism like our family has no chance on its own. I think that's why a lot of family businesses fail."

Dr. Roy Menninger—who works in *his* family business, the renowned Menninger Foundation in Topeka, Kansas—also has thought about the power of the family name, in his case a name that is known worldwide. In the course of his psychiatric practice, Dr. Menninger, who has had lots of experience with conflict in his own family, has counseled a great many members of family businesses who are in conflict.

In a lecture at a Young Presidents' Organization Family Business Conference in Berlin a few years ago, he emphasized the power of a name in terms of its benefits to the individual family member:

"When each of us joins a family, we didn't exactly choose it, but there we are. But when one joins a group, it is because we experience some benefits of membership. Being a member is a way of saying, 'I have a place. I have an identity. I have a connection. I have some value thereby.' Family firms put a great deal of emphasis on this connection, this value of being part of something. The more value associated with the name in monetary terms, the

58

greater the benefit. There are some families with a great deal of money who feel downright aristocratic. The greater the value, of course, the more a family member has to lose, should they be forced out.

"One of the reasons family members often end up in court is that they are wrapped up in the fantasy of name magic. Who carries on the name? As if with the name goes power, quality, wealth, all these wonderful things. Very often women, because they cannot carry on the name or typically don't, feel that they do not even have access to something which these others share."

Dr. Menninger concluded his discussion of the connection between family myth and the family name by saying that both "give meaning to this identity we have with the family business. They justify our dependency. They sustain our loyalty. They do help hold a family together."

Negative Possibilities of the Family Myth

The same myth can have a helpful or hurtful effect on the family in the family business. We already know that businesses and families are not alike. Families are supposed to be supportive and nurturing, and while businesses may offer those benefits to employees, it's not their reason for being.

We also know that individuals can be mean, and greedy, and blindly ambitious. Thinking about succession, and sibling rivalry, and competition for parental affection and approval, it's not hard to imagine a family business scenario in which things go horribly wrong:

- Some heirs want to sell, some don't.
- A second or third wife may become the widow and inherit a lot of stock while caring nothing for the future of the company.
- The younger generation may want to expand in ways that

59

make the still-in-charge founders regret that they ever became parents.
- There may be different views on management style, investment, growth, and marketing.

In fact, there may be as many reasons why families break up the
business, sell out, or end up in court as there are family members
in the business.

The daughter of the heir to one family business, a Northeast real
estate dynasty, said to me during our interview that her uncle, who
runs the family business with her father, regularly sends her newspaper clippings of other families' lawsuits.

"There's a constant stream of paper from him about families
feuding in court," she said. "Or my father would sit me down and
say, 'Listen, let the Binghams be a lesson to you. They'll talk to any
reporter who comes down the pike and tell them the most incred-
ible stories, but they won't talk to each other. This is not the way
loving families behave."

Part of any family's myth may be that people just don't get along.
It's basic psychology that the more you repeat a behavior, the more
you re-enforce it. Have a knock-down argument with your brother
once a week for a year, and that will prove to be a very hard habit
to break once the two of you have reached top management. Perhaps you don't like your brother, but it could also be that you don't
see him accurately because you're living out the older generation's
story by perpetuating conflict. It's often impossible to get people to
look at patterns of behavior, even when history repeats itself again
and again. This sort of family situation frequently can be solved
only by an outside facilitator, who is not personally involved and
can stand back for a fresh perspective.

The intensity of family business conflict has been observed by
Dr. Menninger in his practice.

"Members get caught up in the need to destroy each other as part of the cost of fighting at all," cautioned Dr. Menninger. "There is the inevitability of Greek tragedy in these dramas when a lot of money and power is involved. Lord Russell said a marvelous thing: that people would sooner die killing their enemies than successfully vanquish them. In a family business, many people can be so convinced of their own rectitude and position that rationality no longer reaches them and they would sooner die than change."

If patterns of conflict become the way of life for a family that is in business together, then difficulties are expected and come as no surprise to the participants. Discord takes its place in the family mythology and becomes a burden for the entire family to bear, perhaps for the life of the company.

According to family business consultant Kathleen Wiseman, problems within the family business suffer added intensity because of past baggage that family members bring to any conflict. Separating past problems from present reality often proves an impossible task. Ambiguities resulting from unresolved problems gain momentum over time, and after many years they can pack a serious emotional wallop.

As the same patterns are repeated within a family, the players often assume, and predict, that someone will act in a certain way: "Your uncle Charlie always flies off the handle and fights with the clients," or "Your sister Margaret has never had any sense. I don't think she'll ever be ready to take over a department." These statements are repeated as gospel, leaving little opportunity to change or grow. They become classic examples of a self-fulfilling prophecy. Useful techniques of communicating and conflict resolution too often may remain untested by traditional family businesses, although these techniques are often the only realistic chance these companies have for long-term survival.

61

THE SYMS NAME AND OUR FAMILY STORIES

In my own family business, we have experienced many uplifting and beneficial effects of family stories. We also have experienced the phenomenal power of the destructive side. In fact, there's a definite Old Testament resonance to my father's story.

My father, the youngest of eight, had six sisters and a brother, George, who was sixteen years his senior. When Sy married and started raising a family, it seemed a sensible plan for him to leave an uncertain career in broadcasting to join his brother in his retail clothing store on Greenwich Street in Lower Manhattan. George had inherited the store from my grandfather—the Law of Primogeniture at work.

My Uncle George was a gregarious man, with a glamorous wife and lifestyle. But he wasn't a good manager, and even worse, he was an uninterested buyer. So when George was at the barber's or just taking in an afternoon movie, my father ordered the underwear and socks and kept the customers and the few other employees happy. The great difference in age, almost that of father and son, was matched by differences in personality and temperament. There was little brotherly empathy, and they probably didn't even know each other as friends until much later in their lives.

With this as background, the family story about Syms started when, after several years as an employee, Sy asked Uncle George if he would be willing to sell him part of what was, after all, his father's business.

George agreed to part with 20 percent if Sy could come up with its estimated value in cash. It took him six years to earn the agreed-upon amount—$6,000. Sorry, said George, 20 percent is worth much more than that today. After all, six years had passed. Echoes of the Old Testament, as in Genesis we learn how Jacob worked for

Laban for seven years to win Rachel as his wife, only to be cheated by the secret substitution at the marriage ceremony of her older sister Leah.

But unlike Jacob, who slaved for another seven years to finally earn his bride, my father had had enough. He used the money he had saved and found himself a nonfamily business partner to start his own dream.

In those years, the late fifties and early sixties, the part of Lower Manhattan that now houses the World Trade Center was an area specializing in discount electronics, job lot auction houses, and, because of its proximity to Wall Street, men's clothing stores. And so my father started looking there for a location. A cousin of my father's owned a menswear store around the corner from Uncle George's establishment that he wanted to vacate, so Dad signed a lease and prepared to open.

My father had served many customers during the years that he had worked for Uncle George at Merns—our family's original last name and the name on the store. How were those hundreds of customers to find their way to the new enterprise? In the time-honored way: Dad put his name on a sign in front of the store—SY MERNS.

The volcanic reaction from Uncle George is proof enough of the power of a name. To make matters worse, my father had miscalculated. He didn't have hundreds of customers who wanted to see what Sy Merns had to offer, he had thousands. Fuming from his post at his storefront window, Uncle George called his lawyer.

The next thing we knew, the Merns family had to communicate in the language of lawyers. Our many-faceted, complex family situation was reduced to two dimensions—theirs and ours, and right or wrong—guilty or not guilty.

The battle lines were drawn. Four of my father's sisters, led by the oldest, took Uncle George's side. The other two remained neutral. Spouses and children followed suit and suddenly we had a situation rivaling the Capulets and Montagues. The sides were established and each believed that they were right.

Finally, the issue was taken to the courts. My uncle felt that it was unfair competition for my father to advertise his store as "Sy Merns." The judge agreed, so a compromise was struck. Dad took his first name, Sy, and combined it with the first and last letters of Merns, and arrived at a name that the court would accept.

Eventually, it became simpler for Sy to change his name legally from Merns to Syms, but that was not until he began TV advertising in 1974. Having one's private life scrutinized by lawyers and judges had been a brutalizing experience for my father. As with so many other families whom I've spoken with who have had conflict escalate into litigation, all the participants felt as if they had been betrayed. The experience left wounds that have never completely healed. How the conflict that caused those wounds is interpreted by the next generation tests the elasticity and the commitment to a positive family mythology by all the family members.

I think a recipe for success includes one part creative compromise and two parts effective communication. I truly believe that families can learn to keep the family business machine running if they talk to each other and try to follow an agreed-upon businesslike agenda.

After years of patiently and persistently trying to keep the lines of communication open with his children, my father has negotiated the return of one of my brothers who had left the business. My sister Adrienne, Sy's youngest child, joined Syms after I started working on this book and is contributing very nicely as a women's clothing buyer. Sy's youngest son remains outside the business.

Despite some conflict, I consider my family a success. As more than one person has pointed out to me, the larger the family, the greater the difficulty in achieving total harmony. I had three brothers in the business when I became president of Syms. Only two are currently with the company. But rather than looking for unanimity, I prefer to concentrate on strengthening the bonds that remain.

Some, if not all, of us have learned to communicate with each other in a way that does not tear us apart. We have tried to compromise, and today share a deeper feeling of caring and commitment. We have regular family council meetings where we can air our differences. We look forward to these meetings and we are pleased to see ourselves operating as adults within the family system, not hanging on to, or repeating, old childhood behaviors. I remember something aptly said by one of my interviewees, Nancy Lampton, chairman of her family's third-generation Louisville, Kentucky, insurance business. She described the result of being forged in the furnace of family business conflict as "so much gold after the dross has been burned away."

Chapter

4

Sharing the Room
at the Top:
The Parents' Eye View

Family businesses that are able to continue past the second
generation must have lives of their own. They must be constructed in such a way that they can survive even the retirement
or death of the founder. When such a structure is present, it usually
means that the family managing the business has worked out a way
of living and working in which the good of the business is put first.
It is understood by the family members that when family matters
and business matters conflict, what's good for the business takes
precedence. How the family members relate outside the office
might be another situation entirely.

In any event, that's the way it's *supposed* to work. When I first
started researching this project and approached members of other
family businesses with my initial questions, I had a feeling that

their answers would include many variables. At a Young Presidents' Organization conference a few years ago, small-business consultant Theodore Cohn pointed out that, in his experience, the words "It depends" applied to almost all the rules that govern successful family businesses. I, too, found these words applicable as I talked with family after family. Although there are a great many similarities among family businesses, it is hard to generalize about their structures. Each one truly is different.

How, for example, is your family business constituted?

- Is it a cash cow for the entire family? Is money that might be used for research and development or expansion paid out yearly in dividends?

- Is every child of every sibling welcome to join the family firm at the appropriate age regardless of his or her qualifications? As well as your fifty-five-year-old cousin who still hasn't "found himself"?

- Do you have some sort of training program for younger members of the family who will enter the business? How do you intend to train these young people? At what level will they start and who will supervise them?

- What about nonfamily employees? Are they given a piece of the profit pie and can they count on job security and competitive salaries? Are they trusted?

- Are daughters included when you consider hiring the next generation? Or do you have a "men only" club?

- Are you going to be able to give up control when the time comes? And will you know when that time arrives? Do you have a succession plan in place . . . and what about estate planning?

- Are the members of your family who own the company,

whether or not they work for it, in agreement as to the future direction of the business? Or do you unilaterally make decisions to which everyone else must adjust?

I'm not suggesting that, in the abstract, there's a right or a wrong way to answer these questions. They are not questions concerning right and wrong. I am suggesting that you, whatever your age, ought to ask yourself each of these questions and make sure that a well thought out answer is ready when needed—because for you, in your special situation, there definitely is a right or a wrong answer. The right answer will work well in your business and the wrong answer will not.

In considering the meaning of the phrase mentioned by Cohn, "It depends," I can only say that it depends on family history, the talent of family members in the business, the temperament of those in charge now and those who see themselves as heirs, and the clarity of shared goals.

This chapter is addressed to the parental generation. When I say "you," I'm thinking about people, men or women, like my own father, who, if they are not the founders, might be the founders' children—second-generation heads of companies. You are the leaders who know better than anyone else how all-encompassing, and sometimes ambiguous, those words "It depends" can be.

Rules of behavior and objectives may have existed for centuries, as in, for example, a religious order such as the Catholic Church, or you might be an employee of an enormous multinational operation and have little voice in day-to-day operations. Perhaps you're a colonel in the United States Air Force. If you go by the book, as most successful military people do, then you know pretty much what is expected of you and what you might expect as you move up through the ranks. There are hierarchies on top of hierarchies—changes, even essential ones, have to pass through too many entrenched gates. The changes never occur, but instead die of frustration.

Most businesses don't suffer from these restrictions. The competitive pace is just too fast. There are constantly new opportunities. Today's cutting edge is tomorrow's straight razor. The founder of the family business started something unique, but to survive, it depends on the creativity and talents of those who are in charge. If you own a controlling share of a company that you also manage, then the governing rules are *your* rules, and you had better know what you're about if you want your company to continue into the next generation. It is your job to make sure that the organism that you have either created or inherited can function independently of your moods.

Mistakes to Avoid
Your business plan for the family firm may not go as well as you had hoped. If the business ends before the family is ready to exit, then you will probably consider yourself a failure for not being a better caretaker of your family's business future.

You need to guard against common management mistakes that a great many founder/entrepreneurs commit again and again, yet, being set in their ways, do not recognize. For example, it may be that:

1. You have not set clear management priorities. When business decisions conflict with the wishes of some family members, which take precedence?
2. You have been too insular and don't see the end of a business

cycle. Therefore, you cannot compete properly for tomorrow's market share.

3. Your management style remains unrelievedly autocratic. Your word is law, and you are not interested in dissent from anyone—family outside or inside the business, or nonfamily employees.

4. You don't have a clue about the next generation. You've talked with your kids about coming into the business, but you have no real plan in place to make that a reality. You don't know what they want or even what you want from them.

5. You've never thought about such concepts as communication, flexibility, change, independent advisers, family business councils, and outside board members. And you're certainly not going to think about what might happen if you get sick, or infirm, or incompetent. You'll think about mortality tomorrow.

6. You don't want to set things down on paper because that would confine you and you've worked too hard for the right to change your mind without having to answer to anyone.

7. You can't delegate because no one can do it or understand it as thoroughly as you.

These are certainly the most thorny problems I came across facing the controlling generation. Sooner or later, most family businesses face some of them. Add to these the heart and soul of family business survival: how to get the kids into the business, keep them there, make them productive, and then extricate yourself with good grace and minimal heartbreak when the time comes to leave your creation in the hands of a new generation.

Welcoming the Next Generation

The thing about a family business is that it employs members of a family. These relatives may be your siblings or cousins, or representatives of your parents' generation, and eventually you are going to have to consider the next wave: your children, nieces, nephews, and interested others.

You've had a lot of years to think about these young people. By the time they're of college age, you may have some indications of each person's suitability for, and interest in, your company. But how you bring them in and what you do with them once they're in place are some of the most important business decisions you will ever make. It's your company's future that you're arranging here.

Every field or profession has its "must knows." Among the first things that novice journalists learn are the basic rules of construction for a news story: the lead must contain the information answering the questions who, what, when, where, how and why. It is quite important that before the first offspring appears on your doorstep, you have certain rules and "must knows" in place. These regulations should apply to everyone equally, and can even be codified in writing so misunderstandings can be more easily understood. If you set down guidelines answering the questions who, what, when, where, how, and why, those guidelines ought to cover most contingencies.

Family business consultant David Bork, in a recent article in *Nation's Business* magazine, suggested, tongue-in-cheek, that every family develop a working document like the one he helped write for the "Wilson" family, for their "Golden Goose Company."

Bork wrote: "The purpose of this policy is to define the procedures, processes, and criteria that will govern how Wilson family lineal descendants and/or their spouses enter and exit from the family company's employ. This employment policy is intended to remove the ambiguity that currently exists so that interested family members can shape their career paths accordingly."

In other words, in the Golden Goose working document, expectations of both the employer and the employee are set down, in writing, so that no misunderstandings arise. Topics covered include corporate philosophy, conditions of employment (educational background, work experience, age of applicant, compensation, job application procedures), and succession intentions.

Your success at making your offspring, the job applicant, aware of the rules and "must knows" will forever color your working relationship with your child. And your family's acceptance or rejection of the guidelines that you set down will depend on the perceived purpose of your business. You and your relatives might really believe that the business exists as an employment opportunity for any family member who wants to join. Or a small growth rate might be acceptable to you as long as dividends are paid on schedule.

For the goal of generational continuity to be reached, I believe, the company, no matter what its goods or services, must be run as a competitive entity, engaging in those standard business practices necessary to stay afloat during ever-changing economic times. Such a company must be aggressive. Goals might include gaining a larger market share, keeping creative executives, or learning to compete successfully in the international marketplace. This type of thriving company will incorporate into its managerial ranks only those family members who can contribute something useful to the running of the business.

Who Will Join the Company?
Where do you start? Are your kids going to give you a signal that they're ready to work? Do you make them an offer they can't

refuse? How old should they be before you start thinking seriously about possibilities? How much should you tell them about the business? And, most importantly, are all your children equally welcome to join the company?

Some parents and children are comfortable with each other's ways, and are used to the give and take of intimate relations. These are the families that have shared information about their lives over the years, who have spent a lot of time talking with each other. They have a deep level of trust that underlies all considerations. In my interviews, the word "osmosis" was used frequently by the children of the families that I would include in this general category of businesses that function well.

Lynn Manulis works with her mother, Martha Phillips, founder and owner of Martha's, one of New York City's most prestigious retail dress shops. I discussed the concept of osmosis with her. Growing up, I had heard so much from my father about his business, and had spent so much time at Syms, that when I joined the company, I felt as if I could run a store by myself. And yet I'd never had a day of formal training in retailing. Manulis said: "It's the best kind of apprenticeship. It's been going on your whole life, only you don't realize it. You grow up, and suddenly you've been given this space to work in and you realize you know every nook and cranny. You say to yourself, 'How did I know that? Why did I know that answer?' It's a little bewildering, but somehow you do know."

The first guideline for successfully introducing your children into the company might be: *Know your child.* Don't wait until they're eighteen years old to find out if they have an interest in your paper box company. You might be disappointed to learn that they intend to perfect their talents on the bassoon in hopes of a serious career in music.

The second guideline: *Encourage the process of osmosis.* If you are a member of a family business, it ought to occur to you even when your children are tiny tots that someday you may want one or more of them to join you. Now this may happen or it may not, according to the wishes of your offspring, but it would be foolish not to give the kids all the positive reinforcement that you can. If they have all the information, then they can make an informed decision at the appropriate time. It's possible that the "who" in who should come into the business might take care of itself.

The process of osmosis means that the kids—to say nothing of your spouse—ought to enjoy the privileges as well as the responsibilities of the business. Coming home after a day at the office and saying things about your brother like "That damn so-and-so is always screwing up the orders and . . ." is neither going to contribute much to civilized dinner table chat nor make the thought of joining you in the business very enticing. Your goal is to gradually give your children a realistic view of the company, but do try to share with them a little of the enthusiasm that you feel when things go well—not just the downside when you have to deal with inevitable problems.

Even when they're quite small, take them to the office just to have fun. Little kids like to think that they're helping. Ask them to photocopy something, let them ride on anything mechanical, have ice cream in the cafeteria. Pleasant associations, familiarity with the physical plant, increased understanding as they get older, perhaps a summer job—if you introduce these elements into the lives of your children, you will reap positive benefits later on. And if your kids turn to other interests, at least they'll know what they're missing.

Sam LeFrak is still, in his mid-seventies, chairman of the Lefrak Organization, the mammoth construction and real estate empire, although day-to-day management has passed to his son, Richard.

But Grandfather Sam is already looking to the next generation, and is a great example of how to introduce some fun into a small child's life, while preparing him for the future. One of Sam Le-Frak's habits is to take his young grandson with him on his rounds: the two of them visit real estate sites in the comfort of Sam's limo. The grandchild is introduced to management from the top, spends a day with Grandpa, and Grandpa gets to show off the next generation to employees and business associates. If Sam LeFrak's grandson is not interested in the family business when he grows up, it will not be for lack of grandparental trying.

Sometimes you have to help osmosis along a little bit: that's where some subtle marketing comes in. If you're faced with lack of interest from a young but promising member of the next generation, do a little selling as that child grows up.

You can concentrate on the positives that you've experienced over the years: tell funny anecdotes, present the interesting challenges you've faced, try to pinpoint your audience's interests and see how they can be related to your business. This is a public relation's job—you're selling your company to future management.

The third guideline: *The kids have to* earn *their right—to take their place in your company, and then perform and produce their way to the top.*

The Adolph Coors Company exemplifies this third guideline. A fourth-generation, Colorado-based company that is now the third-largest brewery in the United States, Coors is noted for its tough-minded management policies. *Everyone* starts at the bottom to learn about the business, and promotion is based strictly on merit.

Family Business magazine recently profiled Coors management, interviewing Bill Coors, chairman of the parent company, and his nephew, Peter, now president of the largest subsidiary, Coors Brewing.

Said Bill: "The control here is such that you don't worry about hurting people's feelings. Anyone in the family who wants to can start here at the bottom and work their way up. I had a cousin, about ten years older than I, who graduated college and came to work here. A month went by and it was payday, and there was no paycheck for him. He went in to see my grandfather and asked where his paycheck was. My grandfather said, 'Well, I've been watching your work, and I'm seriously considering charging you for working here.'

"My cousin could have reacted to that in a constructive way, but instead he got mad and quit."

Even though there is no free ride within the Coors family business, a great many members of each generation have been willing to abide by their family's unwritten employment contract—to start at the bottom, work hard, and reap the rewards if they have the ability to compete successfully and produce efficiently.

Guideline number four: *Try to be flexible in your long-term management projections.* Until it actually happens, you don't have a clue as to which, if any, of your kids might come into the company. And once there, of course, they might not stay. Or once having made another career choice, they might decide that the family business offers more attractive possibilities. The only thing that you can count on absolutely is that kids can change their minds. Or things don't work out. Or people disappoint. Or you disappoint people. Or events work out better than expected.

So in thinking about the future, you can only base your planning on the best information available. If you are habitually inflexible, I can suggest unequivocally that consciously trying to introduce a little "give" into your management style will help you stave off trouble—perhaps even heartbreak. As you get older, and the company and you mature, you will *have* to accept change sooner or later. It's in the nature of things. How much easier all around if you've accepted certain inevitabilities and have a new management team in place to make transition easier.

Planning for the future is best done when it's started as early as possible. From the time that your children are tiny, even the remote possibility of having a new generation join you in the company may unconsciously govern some of your business decisions. O. M. "Koke" Cummins is president of Mansfield Industries, in Ohio, a diversified company that specializes in metalwork, plating, and the assembly of mechanical components. At the time that I interviewed him, Cummins had two sons in the business, one of whom had made a firm commitment to the company; the other was still finding his way.

Cummins gave substance to the idea that having a real, live body representing the next generation does heighten an emphasis on planning. Said Cummins: "Of the three children [his daughter, Claudia, works in Washington, D.C.], it's most natural for Bruce [the son who decided to commit to the family business] to want to come into the business, not because he's the oldest but because he's the one that has the most interest. Steve [the second son] rents a farmhouse and has a couple of goats and is married happily and loves his animals, his woodworking, and who knows what he'll do eventually. If we as a family ever found a business for him that really fits, I think we might go into that."

Koke Cummins took over the family business in 1965 and spent the next twenty-five years building the company, enduring a devastating plant fire in 1977 that destroyed almost 85 percent of their production capability. As he says, getting back on his financial feet put the business in a "survival holding pattern to reduce debt in a company that suddenly was not growing any more and had a tremendous debt load that had to be worked out.

"We went through the recession and the markets just fell apart.

During those years, no one else in the family was in the business other than myself. But also during those years, my three children, Bruce, Steve, and Claudia, came along, got older, went away to school or whatever, and exhibited different levels of potential for the business.

"In some areas, I adopted a little bit of a holding pattern while I made a determination as to where I was going to take the business while I waited to see if, in fact, anyone from the family showed an interest."

Eventually, Koke Cummins got the help for which he was waiting.

"Our oldest son, Bruce, had worked in the plant for a summer or two, and then had worked for me for about six months on a specific project when he first got out of college. He then moved to Boston for about two or three years, working in a completely unrelated field. We did have an informal, ongoing dialogue about his eventual interest in coming back into the company. I thought it would be a good choice for him as far as the job went, but I didn't know how he'd like living in Mansfield, Ohio.

"In 1987, an opportunity came along for us to get into a new line of business: the assembly of mechanical components. If we went ahead with it, I would need a separate business framework with labor costs lower than I could manage in my unionized company. We were trying to make a successful bid for business that would otherwise go to Mexico.

"Bruce and I got together the cost projections. It looked good, but I needed someone on the spot to run it. So: 'Bruce, do you want to come home and start a business?' Despite important ties in Boston, he agreed, and, so, with $3,000 we started a completely separate corporation, owned by my three children, affiliated with what I do in my own company. We wanted them separate for legal reasons, potential estate and tax reasons, for labor reasons, and to give the kids something that could grow.

"The company, founded with just $3,000, borrowed money and started production in rented space. Two years later, it was doing just under $4 million. It's now in its fourth year."

My four guidelines for introducing the next generation into the business are successfully brought to life by Koke Cummins and his family. From the start, the business was a family affair, and, as his children have become adults, Koke sees them as unique and separate personalities and seems to accept their career decisions. He remains flexible, leaving room for their inevitable growth and change while he continues to manage a thriving conglomerate. It does seem that he has reaped the reward of having at least one of his children commit to the business heart and soul.

Suggestions for Easy Entry

It is only possible to offer *suggestions* when the question arises of which children are temperamentally suited to come into the family business—there are no absolutes. But here are what I think are a few useful thoughts gleaned from my interviews with the current generation of CEOs:

- All children are not created equal and should not be treated as if they were. Some are smart, some not; some are agreeable, some impossible. Some have a good work ethic, some are flakes. This has nothing to do with your love for them. You can show that love by remembering them all equally in your will, or in various ways during your lifetime. But these remembrances should have nothing to do with the governance of your company. Control ought to go to those who are most competent, and who have earned the right to manage. These people may be your sons or daughters or talented and dedicated nonfamily executives.

- Kids who want to come in should show some sincere interest in the company and what it does. A simple point, perhaps, but you don't want to end up a way station as they try to get their lives in order. If they don't know yet what they're interested in, let them work someplace else first. Your business is not a place to hang out.

  After all, although you want the best for your children, all relationships, whether personal or business, ought to be a two-way street. And you will feel much better about your child if there's a real desire on his or her part to participate productively.

  I told a story recently in the business advice column I write for *Family Business* magazine that, although a well-known joke in business circles, is sometimes all too true.

  A father invites his son, a recent college graduate, to join his business. The father offers the son 50 percent of the company's stock and asks him what area of the business he would like to manage.

  Not the factory, says the son, there's too much physical labor involved. He also turns down positions in marketing, accounting, and all the other departments as well. Nothing seems quite right to him.

  "Well," says the father, now thoroughly exasperated, "you don't want to work in the plant, you don't want to work in the field, and you don't want to work in the office. And yet I've just given you 50 percent of the business. What *do* you want to do?"

  And the son answers: "Would you consider buying me out?"

- Analyze the corporate culture that you have no doubt established by now and with which you feel comfortable. It would not be appropriate for you to bring into your company a child whose lifestyle is anathema to you, or who thinks that you're annoyingly old-fashioned, or whose morals and mores cannot co-exist with your own. Or with whom you just don't get along.

Most of all, you need a little luck. Nothing is harder than saying no to a well-loved but incompetent child who lives to work by your side and is prepared to do nothing else. In this situation, your best bet is to keep the company very profitable so it can support these unproductive hangers-on.

The Sticky Question of Compensation

What about money? You've passed the hurdle of negotiating your child's entrance into the company. What sort of salary should your son or daughter be getting?

Whatever financial arrangement you make with your child, it should be perceived as fair to both of you. Treat your child as you would any other employee. It may be that he or she will have a supervisor other than you, anyway, so the entire subject can be handled through a third person.

Rule of thumb: Pay what you would pay someone who is not a family member. The salary ought to be competitive, related to the general outside job market, and based on your child's educational and work background. In other words, you pay your child what he or she is worth.

Extras and perks should be discussed up front, just as you would do with any new hire. Stock options, bonuses, profit sharing—make sure your child understands the details of these. You don't want any accusations of neglect later on.

Keep in mind that if you are anything less than fair, competitive, and absolutely clear about what your son or daughter can expect in the way of compensation now and in the near future, you run the risk of turning him or her off to the new job before you've even started to work out an arrangement at the office. It's the really talented kids who are turned off the most, and the quickest, if they think they've been treated shabbily. They can always get another job somewhere else, and they will.

The Right Timing

Sylvia Woods has run a world-class restaurant, called simply "Sylvia's," in New York City's Harlem for thirty years. In 1979, food critic Gael Greene enthusiastically referred to her as the "queen of soul food" and the rest is food history—New Yorkers lost her to the world, as thousands of tourists made their way to Lenox Avenue and 126th Street in Harlem. Today, Woods runs the restaurant with the help of her husband, Herbert, and their four children.

Sylvia Woods told me how all the kids were "started off early in the restaurant. But when they grew up, they rebelled. They wanted to get away from the restaurant." Which they did—working for other food establishments, for the City of New York, for lots of other people. But, over time, they all came home to the family's business. Not only are all four allied to the restaurant in some way, but some of the Woods grandchildren are already involved, making it today a three-generation business.

The experience of the Woods family brings to life a recommendation made by almost all my interviewees—a suggestion that I echo enthusiastically.

A guideline: *It is absolutely vital that a member of the upcoming generation who is interested in joining the family business work somewhere else first, and you should urge them to do so.*

I spent several years toiling at various media jobs before I joined Syms, and I never regretted for a minute the experience and self-knowledge that I acquired during those sometimes difficult years. I even know what it's like to be fired.

William Modell, chairman of the board of Henry Modell and

Company, sporting goods retailers, has two sons in the business, each of whom bears the title of president, although their areas of responsibility are quite different.

During my interview with the chairman, I asked him what advice he would give to members of the CEO generation—his generation—when their children first indicate that they might be interested in the business.

"First of all," said Modell, "make sure they start somewhere else, that they don't come from school right into the business. It's very important that they get some experience and make their own mark somewhere else. I think the father develops a lot more respect for the child, and the child will have a lot more confidence in himself, if he is able to make a success somewhere else. I notice that one of the things that's said when someone comes right out of college and into the business is: 'Well, he's there because he's the boss's son.' Everyone then wonders forever if he could have made it on his own."

So when is it the right time for your son or daughter to start working in your business? Now don't hate me for this . . . but it depends. And it depends on:

When they're ready. Never force. As in the case of Sylvia Woods, they may not be interested in your business if they think the grass is greener somewhere else. And: They really *should* try something else first. A child who comes directly into the company has no credentials whatsoever. With no credentials, he or she will garner no respect. Remember one of our first recommendations: If your child does come into the company, he or she should offer something real, something professional, and have some qualifications other than being related to you.

You want your child to have a different perspective gained elsewhere for that child's sake. It can be intimidating coming into a company where your parent is the boss. Other employees will be watching curiously, and some will be waiting for them to fall flat. Successful employment elsewhere, even in an unrelated field, can work wonders in developing self-confidence in your son or daughter. This is the necessary self-confidence and self-respect that they'll need to have as developing professionals, and which they'll need in order to have the strength to disagree with you when appropriate.

Should Your Kid Star at the Bottom?

There are several schools of thought about where in the company your child should start—presuming that you have a business large enough to have departments. It's perfectly possible that you may have the sort of small company in which many hands make light work—your kids will fill in wherever needed. This discussion is not for you.

Should your kid start at the bottom? At the top? Somewhere in between? Most of the founders whom I interviewed did not look to the old ways as necessarily the best ways. They didn't seem to think it too important that their children start in the shipping department and spend years working their way up the ladder to the executive suite.

For one thing, kids today frequently have more formal education than the post-World War II entrepreneurial generation that's retiring now. There's no real reason for a young college graduate and recent M.B.A. to drive a delivery truck for six months. And, yet, it wouldn't be a bad idea for that person to do it for two weeks or to work summers in college as a schlepper. There really is no substitute for doing it yourself. My interviewees did agree that the new employee—especially one who might be groomed for the top job someday—ought to have as much hands-on experience as possible.

Particularly in a company that *makes* something, your child ought to spend enough time in each department so that he or she understands what a manager from these departments is talking about at each stage of production.

Wherever you decide to introduce your child into the company, many of my respondents agreed on what I think is another important guideline: *If at all possible, have your child work in an area where he or she does not have to report directly to you.*

This may not be your dream of working side-by-side with your offspring, but try to be patient. You know this person very well. Remember, you knew your son or daughter as a child and adolescent, when they were, not surprisingly, childish and possibly difficult.

My father addressed this problem in an interview a few years ago: "If the child and the parent are both still in the business, and the parent is the employer and the child the employee, it can be unfair to the child. After all, that parent didn't know any other employee until they were adults. But with your own child, you have a lot of memories. You can remember if they lied to you when teenagers, and that just sits there in your memory bank. You might even wonder if they're lying to you in a work situation, which would probably never occur to you with any other employee. So you can see that a child can be at a tremendous disadvantage."

The best solution, advised my interviewees, was to put a little distance between parent and child in the office. Your children are young adults now, and presumably have left their childish ways behind as they attack their careers. Your goal is now primarily a good working relationship with them.

Even though your offspring may not report directly to you for their first few years with the firm, you must be vigilant and keep an eye on how they're doing. There are signposts that you should watch for as you assess their progress. For example:

- Be sure that you're not setting your children up for failure. Play to their strengths, not weaknesses. They should be given enough autonomy so that they can succeed on their own, but don't throw them in beyond their depth. They should work in areas in which they have some interest, even though it may not be yours. Let them learn something new—a field that will not duplicate your knowledge but rather enhance and complement it.

- Help them find a mentor, or a coach. This should be someone in the company other than yourself who has good will toward your child, and will teach and advise without feeling threatened.

- Make sure their supervisor is someone they respect. This person will be the one to discuss salaries and bonuses, do scheduled reviews, and perhaps even criticize your child's job performance. There is no real reason for you to perform any of these job-related tasks unless you have set up a hierarchy in which your child reports directly to you—which is more difficult to do successfully.

  Henry Bloch—chairman of H&R Block, the country's largest tax preparation company, of which his son, Thomas, is president and CEO—talked with me about his method of communicating discontent to his son: "I contact a third party in our office of the chairman," said Bloch, "and talk to him about whatever it is. He'll tell me what he thinks and then says, 'Well, let me talk to Tom about it,' which he does. I don't want to be critical of my son. Life is too short."

- Make sure that your child's performance is reviewed regularly. A rule of thumb: If your child has worked for the business for three years full-time, and been evaluated over that time, and seems to be making no substantial progress in either learning or productivity, then do both of you a favor and suggest that he or she find employment elsewhere.

And If Things Go Wrong?

If your child just isn't working out, you're going to have to face up to the unpleasant task of firing your very own flesh and blood. Your criteria have got to be the same as you would apply to any other employee: ineptness, absenteeism, personality disorders, substance abuse. This may happen someday to some of you, but the best protection against an inept employee is not to hire them in the first place. If someone seems wrong for your company right from the very beginning, or you recognize flaws that you don't really want to live with, even if this is your son or daughter, the chances of it working out eventually are remote.

The most publicly discussed instance I know where a parent fired a child is worth repeating here:

When Tom Leonard, a third-generation son employed by his father's farm and food business in Connecticut, was in his early twenties and not doing a great job in the business—coming in late two days out of five, for instance—he went to collect his paycheck on Friday and was told by the clerk that his father had taken the check home with him and wanted to see Tom as soon as possible.

Tom went home, thinking pleasant thoughts about a promotion, as that's the way they were awarded in that family business.

His father surprised him mightily by saying: "You know, Tom, being in a family business is really tough. You have to wear two hats. One hat, you're the father, and the other hat, you're the boss. So let me put on my boss hat here for a moment and say 'You're fired.' Now, let me put on my other hat and say, 'Look, I'm really sorry you lost your job. Can I help you in any way?'"

Although that story always gets a big laugh, I'm inclined to think that sort of well thought out and executed incident is pretty rare. Management professor Wendy Handler said that in her interviews of second-generation business people, the response she got when she talked about firing a child surprised her with its vehemence, as if firing were tantamount to banishment. "It was 'Oh, my God, no! That would never happen in our family business.' "

But it does happen, and is sometimes the most merciful solution to a difficult problem. As Robert Matt, chairman of the Ethan Allen and Workbench furniture companies, told me: "Don't *ever* hire anybody you can't fire."

And If Things Go Right

To know why you want your children in the business, you might as well try to figure out the meaning of life. Your family is precious to you. Blood does run thicker than water and can act as a binding agent when you need support. You want to infuse your business with the same strengths, the same loyalty, and the same energy that you, at least ideally, enjoy in your home life.

We know that there are additional complexities and stresses in family businesses. We know that problems at home can affect office life, we know that it's hard to separate your parental hat from your boss's hat, and we also know that if anything goes wrong at the office, it can have a horrendous effect on your personal life.

Nevertheless, you find that you want to enjoy:

- Real loyalty at the office. Your family is, after all, your family. You all have each other's interest at heart. You trust each other.
- The energy that the new generation is bringing to your business. They know state-of-the-art technology and techniques. They can relate to the younger customers, and they have

originality and creativity that don't come easily to your generation any more.

- A sense of immortality. You realize that it's possible your creation will outlive you and continue for the benefit of those you love.
- The reliable help from trustworthy people that perhaps you didn't need when you were younger, but which you accept gratefully now. It's important to you to have your children by your side, sharing the burden. You feel a sense of community, and new strength to keep on going.

YOU CAN CREATE HARMONY IN YOUR FAMILY BUSINESS

I have always liked lists of dos and don'ts. They help me to organize my thinking on a particular subject. In contemplating the complicated elements that foster harmony in any family business, I think the dos and don'ts can be limited to just a few. They're not hard to list but they're terribly hard to follow:

1. Do treat your children in the business as if they were grownups—which, in fact, they are.
2. Do behave toward your children with the same courtesy and attention that you would give a nonrelated employee.
3. Do be clear in your instructions. Let your children know what you want. Make sure that they know if a task is completed to your satisfaction.
4. Don't meddle in their personal lives, especially if you're not asked for advice. On the other hand, set boundaries. You should try to keep family problems in the home, where they belong.
5. Do pay them what they're worth: not too much, not too little. Compensation should relate to the open market.

6. Do give them a helping hand within the company. Try to assign them tasks that are not beyond their capabilities, and that they might even enjoy. If they can bring fresh thinking to a problem, so much the better.

7. Don't let jealousy into your relationship with your children. The mere fact of their being old enough to work in the business means that you're approaching another stage in your life. Try to accept this as the natural course of events.

8. Don't equivocate when it comes to planning their futures— and yours. Your children should know what to expect as they become more expert and capable of more responsibility. If a succession plan is not in the works, it should be. The same is true of estate planning.

9. Do be flexible, but hold your children accountable for results. With the introduction of kids into the company, you have lost a certain amount of control over events. You can neither control their actions nor their thinking. But they must be aware that they are accountable to you, "the boss," and answerable to the company as a whole.

10. Most important: Do talk with your children. The successful family businesses all have a structure for communication. It may be informal—a cup of coffee in the morning, or a rundown of problems as you commute together. Or formal—twice-a-week meetings during which you can talk about anything.

Consider the family retreat, which can take place in a vacation atmosphere. These off-site periods of communication can energize your relationships and foster familial trust.

Whatever format is most natural to you, just do it.

I guess that anyone who manages to follow the above guidelines would be more perfect than is humanly possible. But striving is not impossible. It always helps to have some outside input, too, just to let you know how you're doing: a trusted executive, an old friend, your lawyer, a spouse, or, best of all, your outside, independent board members. Fairness, flexibility, accountability, strategic planning, estate planning, working communications, and careful listening should always appear on your daily checklist for creating the company that you want the next generation to inherit.

Chapter

5

Ready or Not . . .
The Next Generation

In writing this chapter, I was thinking about the toilers in the
family business vineyards who are members of my Baby Boom
generation—or even a little younger. Most of us work for those in
the founder/entrepreneurial group who have been running their
companies, which they perhaps founded, for a long time. The older
CEOs are now facing retirement, as well as the relinquishing of
power to us, their children. And the younger CEOs, although not
ready to consider the Sun Belt, have probably been firmly in charge
for so long that "consensus" and "compromise" are not usually the
two words that spring first to mind in describing them.

So what does that mean for you—the upcoming management
generation? Should you even want to join your parents in the
workplace? After having earned hard-won independence, do you
really need to return to their supervision as adults, or would it be
better for you to choose an occupation far removed from their

spheres of control? In other words, what would be in your own self-interest?

Once again, it depends . . .

1. *On the kind of priorities that you have as a family.* Do you, as a family, agree that the running of the company should provide the greatest good for the greatest number? And are those in charge willing to make the important decisions to ensure the company's success? For instance, are family members welcomed to the management ranks based solely on merit—or clearly exhibited potential? And are you all willing to hire efficient nonfamily management if it seems indicated? If the company is not what you want, is there a forum for discussion? Is there a way in which to sell off equity to support nonworking family members should you want to?

2. *On the emotional relationships that have been formed in your family.* It would seem clear that the sort of behavior involving shouted accusations of betrayal between your father and his sister, or deep-seated animosities dating back to something that was said between parents and children in 1956, do not lay the groundwork for steady-as-she-goes interaction once you all get into a pile at the factory.

Your family has its share of foibles, I'm sure, and it's not reasonable to expect your father, or mother, or uncle always to have the tranquil spirit of a Buddhist monk or the all-knowing knowledge of hindsight. But it is reasonable to expect those at the top to come to some sort of sensible agreement once the smoke has cleared.

3. *On the sort of family culture that you have all developed.* Is there a sense of cohesiveness—and has there always been? And do you feel comfortable with the kind of moral tone that filters down from top management?

If your family works well, both within and without the business, there is enough goodwill floating around to ensure emotional satisfaction and philosophical compatibility concerning the future course of the business.

4. *On the proven talent and adaptability of the generation currently in charge.* If your Uncle Charles is CEO of the family business, and has not changed his mind about anything ever, and two of your older cousins have already tried to work with him and failed, it is not going to work for you either, should you choose to accept his offer of employment.

It doesn't matter that your own father—Uncle Charles's younger brother and second-in-command—has worked with him more or less easily for the past twenty-five years and would like you to come in. They have their own intragenerational relationship, and sometimes the understanding that exists between contemporaries just doesn't translate across generational lines.

Take a leaf from your cousins' notebooks and look elsewhere for employment, at least for now.

And, most importantly:

5. *On the way that your nuclear or extended family typically manages passage through the various stages of life.*

For example, will you as a recent employee be treated as a contributing adult? With ideas and talents of your own, perhaps developed at another company? Or will you always be thought of as a member of the baby generation, forever perceived as little "Willy" by your family when everyone else in the world has known you as "Bill" since your junior year in high school?

Obviously, you cannot possibly know all the answers. But there is one thing I have learned absolutely, drawing on my own experience and that of my interviewees: behavior is the only thing that matters. Promises are just so much lip service. We are what we do, not what we say. It's true that behavior can change, but it takes time, it's painful, and it requires the recognition that change is needed.

If you, for example, have an extremely autocratic parent, who still treats you as if you were a small child and in addition is quite set in his or her ways, the prognosis for you being allowed to strut your stuff to your satisfaction is not good. It would probably be best for you to try to find your way somewhere else for the moment, and perhaps forever. Situations do change over time . . . but usually only over time.

I don't for a minute think that successful families get along all the time. And serious problems with relationships will sometimes arise —certainly they have in my family. But if two things are present —a primary relationship within the business that *does* work, as well as agreed-upon structures for airing grievances—then a family business can usually manage to bandage emotional wounds expertly enough for business as usual to prevail.

"He Made Me an Offer I Couldn't Refuse"

Some family members come into the business because there seems to be no pressing reason not to—for example, you get on pretty well with your father, who is usually the person in charge, and he's enjoyed his work over the years. Why not give it a try?

Before you make a final decision, ask yourself some additional, quite specific, questions:

- *Do you have at least some interest in what the family business does? Or in some aspect of the job?* Perhaps it's the theory of marketing that fascinates you. If that's the case, it may not make too much difference that you manufacture basketball equipment even though basketball is not your sport. You're going to enjoy selling that equipment worldwide.

- *Do you have the stamina for hard work?* You are not going to succeed in the family company if you don't make a serious commitment to it in both time and energy. Other people in the company have made that commitment, and you need their respect.
- *Are you prepared to have others in the company think that you got your job just because you're related to the boss?* Some coworkers are always going to think that, and there's nothing you can do about it. If you have worked elsewhere and learned skills that may not be part of the repertoire of others in the company on your level, then you have a better chance of earning respect from the resident skeptics.
- *Will you be able to take direction from your parents?* This is, after all, not your company yet. You're going to have to learn from them, and be patient, and willing to listen.

My interviewees had all kinds of reasons for coming into their families' businesses, but most joined willingly and enthusiastically. The ubiquitous experience with osmosis comes up again and again: kids grow up with a business, get used to it and its ways, and the idea of having a company to join with which they have a solid connection may seem very attractive.

Michael Modell, of the sporting goods retailer Henry Modell and Company, shares the title of president with his brother, Mitchell. I heard comments similar to his from many of the members of the upcoming management generation: "I would say that the reason my brother and I gravitated to the family business was really twofold," said Michael. "First, we saw that our father enjoyed it very much. He got a lot of pleasure from it—the business always seemed to have affected our father in a positive way. The other major reason was the fact that he never tried to thrust the business on either one of us. It was always, you do what you want to do and be the best you can be at whatever. So our career was left up to us."

Some children are a little less sanguine about proving themselves on the battlefield where a parent is directing the troops. Christie Hefner, chairman and CEO of Playboy Enterprises, the company founded by her very high-profile dad, Hugh Hefner, had a background in journalism, but had not thought seriously about the Playboy organization being a possibility for her. Said Hefner: "I went to college at a very liberal liberal arts university in the early seventies and, quite frankly, a career in business of any kind was not something that I'd given any thought to. It was simply not a possibility for liberal arts educated kids of my generation.

"Of course, I knew what business my father was in, but I had very little sense of what 'the company' was. I knew it had hotels and clubs, but I had no idea at all of the sorts of jobs that people in the organization held, that sort of thing. I was very apprehensive about going into business. Everyone I knew had gone into law, or medicine, or journalism.

"I joined the organization because—and I'm thinking about that great line from *The Godfather*—my dad made me an offer I couldn't refuse. . . . How could I say no? I didn't think of it as the beginning of a five-year plan. I thought of it as an extraordinary opportunity to improve skills and learn about arenas and people and ideas I otherwise would not have access to."

Not all kids, of course, are interested in the family business—some are not interested in any business at all. Kids are kids no matter what decade they're growing up in, and some rebel against everything their families stand for as a matter of pride and rite of passage. And those families, who understand all too well that profits are not a birthright, either have to talk sense to their errant relatives—a ploy that usually does not work—or wait for them to settle down, or forget about them entirely in the business context.

One *Fortune* 500 founder whom I interviewed described his son's early twenties as "the crazy period," when he wanted to be a professional polo player: "I talked him out of it after letting him do his own thing for a while," this founder told me. "I think all kids go crazy from about eighteen to twenty-five. I was a little wild and woolly and hard-headed at that age, too."

Many members of the Baby Boom generation said the sixties for them was a time of total rebellion and rejection of their parents' values. William Kohler, head of the family's bathroom fixture company, told me he went through a mildly wild phase during his college years:

"My father and I didn't associate much during that period. After I graduated from Yale, he and I had a chat about the business. One of my greatest concerns was the depiction of me as the future heir. It was the last thing in the world that I wanted to happen at the time."

Others, myself included, didn't rebel so much as aspire to goals that would fulfill my parents' dreams. There was a time in my young adulthood, undoubtedly influenced by my parents, both of whom had had careers in radio before I was born, when I wanted nothing more than to host a talk show. But we all get older, and experience more of the reality of life. I certainly don't yearn for that now, but if I hadn't worked in television myself—which I did, behind the scenes—and encountered the day-to-day demands and rewards firsthand, I'd probably still be pining.

As a little girl, during the late forties, Bernadette Castro appeared on TV in her dad's commercials, easily opening his convertible sofas. Today she runs the company founded by her father, Bernard, who died during the summer of 1991.

Like the dad of the would-be polo star, Bernadette Castro understands her sons' dreams of a suitable career. She also suffered a show business phase in her early twenties:

"My parents thought it was truly outrageous, but they let me get show business out of my system, and I learned a lot from the experience. I went through it and it was my choice to give it up. Will I let my sons go around the world to surf and make a surfing movie? Probably not, although that would make their lives complete at this point. They're very normal boys. One wants to own a marina. I tell him, 'Fine. Get your law degree and then I'll help you find a place and finance it.'"

It's hard to know what would happen if a parent really wanted to stop a child from doing something they were set on. Could they do it? What would be the benefits? And the fallout? Among my respondents, the feeling was usually a wait-and-see approach, especially if there was interest in having the child come into the business. That child was usually given time to spread his or her wings away from the family business.

Some parents who want their children by their sides win, and some lose. And, sometimes, if the older generation has the patience and can wait long enough, kids do an about-turn and realize that coming home to the family business is not such a terrible idea after all.

COMING INTO THE FOLD

Even though each person's reasons for joining the family firm are different, I can extrapolate certain positive elements that my more contented interviewees seem to share:

- They were not forced into the company by parents trying to make them feel guilty. Free choice reigned.

- They were ready to settle down. Most of them had had other jobs and could see that working for the family company might have attractive advantages.
- They truly wanted to help. There were strong feelings binding together many of these families: no one wanted to be part of the generation that saw the family business self-destruct.
- They saw that within the business a career could be created that would use their talents and fulfill their ambitions.

I don't remember thinking that it would be an especially good idea for me to join my father's business when the time came for me to do *something* work-related. I was, of course, used to Syms—summer jobs, listening to Dad talk about his company at home. The details of Dad's retailing business were definitely an integral part of my impression of the workplace in general.

But Sy never offered me a place at Syms when I reached the age of employment—I don't think he looked and found me wanting. It just wasn't his style to press me unless I wanted him to, and he instinctively knew I wasn't ready to be pressed.

As I progressed through adolescence and young adulthood, I definitely followed my own interests. I went to college, majoring in English, and then earned an M.S. in public relations from Boston University. I always had been interested in broadcasting, and after working as a paralegal for a New York State prosecutor, I followed my natural bent into entertainment, first as an assistant to the president of a radio station in New York City and then as associate producer for a TV talk show.

But associate producers are expendable, and I found out what it was like to be caught up in a cost-cutting campaign. I was out more than once and had to find something else to do.

I certainly hadn't learned everything I needed to know about the communications business, so I took some courses in media sales and combined the study with free-lance projects in market research.

My parents were not living together by this time, and I kept in touch with my dad by having dinner with him every few weeks. During one of these get-togethers in 1977, he told me that he and his right-hand person, who acted as his sounding board, were thinking of expanding, and perhaps would choose a market outside New York. This would be quite a departure for Sy, who was a real New York retailer, and knew the five boroughs inside-out.

Sy had found a community that was cushioned on both sides by the two highest per-capita income markets in the United States. It was the Washington, D.C., area, and the site for this new Syms store would be in Falls Church, Virginia.

I didn't have a full-time job at the time, and it seemed natural for me to offer to go to Washington and work with him preparing an advertising and media plan. Syms had been a TV advertiser since 1974, and Sy carefully educated me on his successful use of the medium. I researched the Washington area, and after three or four weeks proposed a buying schedule for the local media.

By that time I was thoroughly enmeshed in the business of Syms, and I was enjoying myself. When I returned from Washington and Sy asked me what my plans were, I had my answer ready: "I'd like to work at Syms full-time."

In March of 1978, I was ready to make the kind of commitment to Syms that I probably could not have made before. I think the company and I were ready for each other:

- First, Syms could expand. The off-price apparel business had potential for growth in many markets and Sy was willing to try as long as his existing stores remained profitable.

- I had held several jobs and I knew what the work world was like. I knew about the long hours, and lack of recognition for women, and the uncertainty of job security.
- I could offer something to the company. I had job experience, and I had skills. I also had some self-confidence, and was pretty certain that I could master any techniques that I needed. After all, I had been familiar with the business through osmosis since childhood.
- I cared about the future of the company, for both personal and financial reasons. I was very fond of my father, and admired him tremendously. I wanted to help him, and I thought I could learn something from him, although I also knew that he, like most entrepreneurs, was a notoriously bad teacher.

I've worked at Syms for almost fifteen years now. I still look at my job barometer every six to nine months. Sometimes I think that I'm in the wrong business, that I can't stand retailing another minute, or that I'm never going to get the systems working exactly as I want them. But these moments pass, and mostly I'm sanguine and challenged, and don't regret casting in my lot with my father and siblings. The satisfactions that I've experienced at Syms would be very difficult to duplicate in another setting where the personal stakes are not as high.

"CAN'T YOU UNDERSTAND . . .": THE GENERATION GAP

Some family members get along, and others don't. You may have a sister or brother who is your best friend, and another whom you hardly ever think about kindly. That's all a result of individual personality, and family dynamics, and just plain likes and dislikes . . . or a piece of wisdom from my grandmother: "People are born with chemistry, and you can't fight that. It brings them together or tears them apart."

But when you're dealing with your parents' generation in a family business, you just can't afford to ignore generational differences, because they're going to exist. People are different for lots of immutable reasons: sex, culture, religion or race, and—not the least important—age.

I've usually seen the average family business as having an older generation, the parental generation, at the top of the management pyramid, but you could, in fact, be acting out another scenario. *You* could be the founder—perhaps you started a small bakery—and your mother could work for you in any one of a hundred different ways. The usual parent/child roles are then reversed, at least financially. A great deal of sensitivity is required in this case not to upset the natural order of things.

Respect for our elders is not as deeply rooted in the dominant culture in the United States as it is in some other countries and cultures. But it does exist—witness "Honor thy father and thy mother"—and we are in any event hard-pressed to rebel against the older generation in the family business for a lot of reasons, some moral, some ethical, some financial—as well as the sobering fact that they probably own a controlling interest in the company.

The behavior of a person is not always predictable. You may come into the family business to find your parent a model of open-minded flexibility, but they are products of a different time and there is at least the chance that, in an office situation, your mother or father will be:

- *Autocratic.* This person has been running things his or her way for a long time. Problems of jealousy could arise, as in the old buck and the young buck. Your parent, unconsciously resisting change, may even set you up for failure.

- *Old-fashioned.* As in, the old ways are the best ways. You are coming in as a well-educated hotshot. You probably have worked somewhere else, and you have new ideas. Well, once again, it's not your company yet. Try to be tactful. You may find that you still have something to learn.

Most of the younger generation whom I interviewed used the same technique when it came to trying to change a parent's mind: the drip-by-drip approach. Using this tried-and-true method, you make a suggestion, get shot down, and try again later . . . and again . . . and again.

For example, as of now, we offer a Syms credit card, but do not take any other major plastic. My father's theory always has been that Syms offers such good value that the "educated consumer" will recognize that value, and plan ahead when shopping at Syms.

But today we have competition from other off-price chains that we didn't have ten or fifteen years ago, and they accept the usual credit cards. Cards are just more widely used than they used to be—some people will leave the house with a wide selection and not bother with cash or a checkbook.

My dad is boss, and, ultimately, we at Syms will do what he wants to do. He does not want us to accept national credit cards. He feels strongly that only a cash-and-carry philosophy is consistent with an off-price bargain. Will he change his mind? Maybe. But he'll have to see the reasons for himself.

- *Averse to risk.* Things might be too comfortable, or, as my father often tells me when we have a difference of opinion, "We're all eating and we have a roof over our heads," implying that there's no reason to rock the boat with new ideas.
- *Totally wrapped up in the company, with no life of his or her own.* I know of a shirt manufacturer of the old school who, until he died some years ago, still insisted on having his "boys"

105

(the corporation's top executives, most of whom were nearing retirement age) meet with him every morning at about 7:00 to go over the day's plans. The office was in Manhattan, where this founder/entrepreneur lived, but all of his executives had long since moved to the suburbs. No one was too fond of having to leave his house while it was still dark because the CEO was anxious to start another twelve-hour workday.

And yet this custom persisted until the old man died. His business was his life. He was willing to spend as many waking moments as possible absorbed in its affairs, and he expected his management team to be equally involved.

- *Stuck and stagnant.* The problem of the older, "plateaued" owner is quite common: in this scenario, nothing much changes—not the product, nor the customer or client, nor the key employees. New proposals are not usually heeded, which can be very frustrating to the upcoming generation, and growth is rarely a priority.
- *Unwilling to face the passage of time.* At Syms, we have devoted a lot of energy during the past few years to estate planning. But not every CEO is willing to look into the future to deal with estate planning or make sensible succession plans against the day when he or she might retire or die or become incapacitated.

It's so much easier to deal with these thorny matters when everyone is feeling hale and hearty and retirement is not around the corner. A succession plan can be in place for twenty years, but it ought to be in place. When it is not, and something unexpected happens, businesses can collapse or perhaps have to be sold to pay the estate taxes.

Differences between the generations ought not to be news to you, however. After all, you grew up dealing with these differences every day. This older generation is *your* older generation, and you probably understood their particular family ways long before you ever set foot in the company store. That's the thing about families —you know them and how they are likely to react to an idea or situation.

Be Prepared and Anticipate

A guideline that applies to you no matter what stage of life you are passing through is: *Always be prepared for the next step.*

You wouldn't be looking through this book if you weren't thinking at least a little bit about how your career was going, so I must assume that you're willing to invest serious time and effort into figuring out along what lines your own self-interest lies.

If you're one of the lucky ones who has a family business to go into, and you've always wanted to do so, then you can make sure that you arrive at its doorstep with the correct academic credentials. Unless you want to work in the lab at your family's cosmetics company, a general, rather than specialized, education will probably be more useful. But if your family runs a paper mill, then you should at least be conversant in the language of trees. Or, speaking of languages, learn a little Japanese, French, Italian, German— whatever is relevant to your business.

Dealing with the Other Side of a Good Thing

Because I'm speaking to groups more and more on the subject of family business, as well as writing a quarterly advice column for *Family Business* magazine, I keep clips and quotes that I find relevant and that I think will inform or amuse my audiences. Nothing, not even limericks, is off-limits, and I enjoyed the following, which I had stuck in a folder with more weighty material about the problems that could come up in a family business:

107

"Work for me," said the boss, his dad.
"You'll have chances that I never had.
Life served up on a platter,
Your talent's no matter,
And I'll drive you entirely mad."

If you're willing to hang on a cross,
If you're looking to live at a loss,
If your idea of fun
Is to be overrun—
Be the daughter or son of a boss.

There once was a lad name of Wayne,
Who worked for his dad—what a strain.
But he gamely stuck to it,
Tried to guts his way through it,
And now he's completely insane.

Although my interviewees did not turn to verse, each had a list of things that they had found not so pleasant in their association with the family business, and some items on the lists were unique. But many were the same, and repeated again and again—so often, in fact, that you had better be wary of them. My walk on the downside would include:

1. You may find it almost impossible to shake your little-kid image. As a great many fathers have admitted, it's very hard to forget all the stupid stuff that kids without fail have done over the years, even when the offspring shows up bright and early and ready to work. Be businesslike in the office and do not encourage your parent to tell amusing sandbox tales about you if he or she is so inclined.

2. You find it's hard to separate family and home life, especially

if you are close to your parents, siblings, and so forth. You may find that you talk business almost all the time—at the office, at dinner, during a drive in the country. Some families thrive on this, but if you don't, make your wishes known and try to set aside some social situations during which business is not mentioned.

3. You've been working for the family business for a year and you suddenly realize that you haven't been out to a movie in months. Is workaholism part of your corporate culture? You also may be driven, and feel most comfortable in a setting in which you are expected to put in superlong hours. If you don't, you might try to analyze if it's really necessary, but it may be that this company is simply not for you. The fit between family member and company culture basically can be at serious odds.

4. You have no privacy. You may not want, for example, the first question that you hear in the morning at work to come from your mother in the treasurer's office, asking where you were the previous night because she tried to call you three times.

5. If you are the child of the boss, you may suffer from an odd double-edged problem, which might be described as, you can't win, so don't even try. Others are going to criticize you for no reason other than you are the boss's kid. How else could you possibly have gotten the job? That's why it's good to bring as much outside expertise to the company as possible, but even that sometimes is not enough. In addition, it may be almost impossible to get an honest appraisal from anyone. Not your parent, who may feel uncomfortable, and not your superior, who won't want to offend your parent.

The most successful families have gotten around this by treating the relatives just as they would any other hire, with regularly scheduled evaluations and written critiques. When this system works best, the child, even if heir apparent, has a pretty good idea what kind of job he or she is turning in.

6. You will make mistakes, and will just have to suffer through them. William Modell, chairman of Henry Modell and Company, and father of Michael and Mitchell, each of whom has the title of president in the company, told me how sensitive he is about the subject of making mistakes: "I remember what it did to me. My father would get so infuriated if I made a mistake. If I did something stupid, he'd blow up and yell, even if we were on the selling floor. I made a whopper of an error early in my career, involving a U.S. government surplus bid that my father was not enthusiastic about making. But I didn't realize that the amount of the order translated into box cars of an item, and the company had no warehouse space to store it, costing us a lot in trucking and storage fees.

"My father didn't let me forget about that for years. It was such a humiliating experience that I wanted to make sure I treated my sons differently. Of course, if I see them walking off a cliff, I'm going to stop them, but I want them to see what happened to me as an opportunity to learn from their mistakes."

7. You may, as several of my respondents did, feel a great sense of obligation to your parents, and consider yourself almost morally bound to remain in the company. The sense of being trapped can be real, and is usually enervating and frustrating. If you absolutely hate your job, and see no reason why it should ever improve, you really do owe it to yourself to think about leaving. In the long run, it will be kinder to both generations.

If you decide to leave, and your family has not established a pattern for graceful exits, you may encounter a lot of animosity from family members still with the company. Do you think that you're too good for the family business? That's what they're going

110

to think, no matter what the truth underlying your departure.

Remember, too, that once you get into the outside job market, you may find that it is hard to find a comparable position with another company if you present a resume that includes only employment with a family business. A potential employer really has no way of evaluating your skills, or determining whether your job with the family firm entailed real responsibility.

8.   You will feel a lot of anxiety in joining your family business that you will have to deal with, either on your own or with the help of a support group or therapist. Or you might be lucky and have the kind of family, somewhat unusual, that talks things out and addresses individual fears in detail.

Some of the things you might worry about:

- *Failing on the job.* Can you ever follow in your parent's footsteps? Do you even want to?
- *Losing your identity if you stay with the family firm.* You're not sure that you really want to be one among many bearing your family's name.
- *Achieving respect—from your family and other coworkers.* Will your father ever treat you as a colleague?
- *Family relationships.* Will joining the family firm completely change the good feelings that exist between you and your siblings? Does your family deal well with conflict or do you have to be extra vigilant to avoid permanent rifts?
- *The future of the company.* Can you trust the family business to take care of you and your family financially? Does current management have the energy and creativity to plan for decades to come?

I can't tell you not to worry—there's often a great deal to worry about. But this is the only life that you're going to have—you want job satisfaction, and good human relationships, and a little fun, as well. If you have problems at work, which you will, try to address them right away. Difficulties that cause the most trouble are those that fester and grow.

Once again, communicate. Talk with your family. And if you have a problem that can't be solved easily, do what unions are sometimes forced to do: submit to binding arbitration. Get an outside opinion. Your main goal is to achieve a working atmosphere in which you are actually able to work, not worry about an escalating feud with your cousins and aunt.

Think Realistically

It's not a good idea to join a family company with your own hidden agenda. One of the attractive things about such a business is that you're all supposed to trust one another—that's what makes it all worthwhile.

But—you should consider your own self-interest from time to time:

1. *Establish a network of allies.* These may be coworkers on your level. It's good to get input from someone other than top management, or perhaps an older mentor, ideally a person who has no ax to grind and is willing to help you over the rough spots.
2. *Try to develop skills that might be complementary to those of your parents.* How much more efficient to add something new to the company, rather than to duplicate the same tired old experiences, which will no doubt lead to the same tired old solutions to problems. Thomas Bloch, son of Henry Bloch, founder of H&R Block, the world-renowned tax-preparation firm, has managed to do both. He feels that his skills are similar to those exhibited by his father, but, in addition, "I think there

are some differences, too, and in many cases we complement each other." It's a winning combination, and in March 1992 Henry paid Tom the final compliment by naming him chief executive.

3. *Don't forget to keep yourself marketable.* Keep upgrading your skills. Take technical courses, seminars, fill in the gaps in your academic background. This applies whether you intend to stay with the family business for the rest of your life or not. Businesses do fail, or a situation turns sour—you want to be able to jump ship if it becomes necessary.

4. *While you're educating yourself, learn to be a boss.* Being an employee does not teach you to be a manager, which is something that a mentor might help you learn. You need to develop effective administrative and human relations skills, even if you're not going to supervise anyone for a very long time. Be prepared.

5. *Outgrow your childish ways.* Don't lose your temper even if your parent is driving you crazy. It sometimes takes all of a person's willpower to see oneself in the guise of the adult employee, not a naughty six-year-old. Along with this goes acceptance of criticism. Don't sulk. Other employees have to take it— so do you.

6. *Try to impress your adult personality on the older generation.* It is hard for them to see you as other than their child. The technique that works best is a demonstration of new knowledge. After all, most of your life experiences have not been shared with your parents for a very long time.

7. *Humility is not much admired in our country, but when you join the family business, it's good to learn its meaning.* This is not yet your company—others have worked very hard, with clear-sighted intent, to construct the sort of company with which they

feel comfortable. Maybe someday you can put your imprint on it, but not yet.

8.   *Insist on a real job.* This involves a written job description, a supervisor, and goals. Also make sure that your salary and benefits are fair. You don't want to be underpaid, and you want to give real value. It's the only way you will gain the respect of your family and coworkers, and the only way you can assure a solid future with the company.

9.   *Think of the comment that what goes around, comes around.* Nowhere is this more true than in the workplace. People are going to be aware of you just because of your name. If you are tactless, or throw your weight around, or are generally adversarial, coworkers whom you will eventually need will not like you, nor trust you, nor support you. Remember, too, never to attack personally—stick to the idea alone. These are lessons that should have been learned at the playground, but if they have not, pay heed, and learn to share your marbles.

10.   *Work on your relationships with your immediate family if they're with you in the business.* Communicate, try not to be too sensitive, avoid unnecessary conflict, let the relationships grow and mature. These are among the people closest to you—you want the ties that bind you to them to be close and satisfying, and to last a lifetime.

11.   *Update your career goals to reflect your changing stake in the company.* Your needs, and expectations, will change over the years as your position in the company alters. You may have to point out to the company heads your growing expertise and ability to produce. When you know someone as well as they know you, you might find yourself overlooked or not taken seriously, which probably would not happen to a nonfamily employee. Don't be afraid to blow your own horn when necessary

and be clear about what you want and think you deserve. You may not get it, but at least your wishes will be known.

Now . . . for Your Payoff

If all goes smoothly and you establish a comfortable niche within your family's company, then you may find the rewards considerable. I truly believe that there is *nothing* more satisfying than working for a family business that is a functioning unit, one that manages to identify its problems and works with them, always keeping the greater good of the company firmly in sight.

What benefits might you enjoy?

1. Security—emotional and financial. You will be spending your work time with those who ostensibly love you the most and whom you know best. In addition, you will probably be fairly reviewed when raise time comes around. I like to think that no matter whether man or woman, in a family business you get honest pay for an honest day's work.

2. A comfortable feeling of identification with the corporate culture. This is your family, and you know how they think. You probably are very much on their wave length, with shared memories, and family myths, and ties of affection. You all know what you're talking about as you try for the common good.

3. You usually can count on your family. In general, they will have your best interest at heart and will be supportive of your progress. They are not out to get you.

4. Finally, if relationships are progressing smoothly, assume good will. The Golden Rule still applies: Life is easier when you do unto others as you would have them do unto you.

Chapter

6

Daddy's Little Girl

Recently, a friend who haunts secondhand bookstores showed me a copy of a title called *Feminism: Its Fallacies and Follies,* written by a "Mr. and Mrs. John Martin," and published by Dodd, Mead in 1916. Rights for women were a hot subject in 1916—in just four years women would have the vote—and the Martins had a lot to say about women in the workplace: "Humanism recognises that it is impossible in nature for a woman at the same time to bear and rear children and to drain her strength in an outside occupation. Either child or business must suffer. Sensitive women with a natural love for their children abandon the business; tough-minded women, wedded indissolubly to their money-making, let the children suffer. Unfortunate mothers, compelled by poverty to continue at work, know that their children are neglected, and heartbreak at home is added to physical exhaustion at work."

The Martins had a great deal more to say: a woman's natural talent lay in homemaking, they believed, and physical labor and long hours were beyond her strength; it was a man's right and

117

responsibility to care for his family—he was the natural breadwinner; and, most importantly, "when a group of men engage in conversation their minds may be observed to jog along side by side, hour after hour, in the same general direction on the same general topic. But women's minds seem to move rather in curves and circles . . . following lines more beautiful, perhaps, but more irregular and more disconcerting. And thus it arises that when one woman's mind comes in contact with other women's minds, all equally erratic in their orbits, there results a certain mutual bewilderment."

Although the better part of a century has passed, every word written by the Martins can find its supporters today.

There are familiar statistics concerning women's place in the workforce that we all have heard again and again, but I don't think that they can be repeated too often:

In 1960, fewer than 20 percent of mothers with preschool children worked outside the home. Today, almost 60 percent do. Looking even farther back, to 1950, we learn that women comprised about 20 percent of the total labor force; today, they account for more than half of all working Americans, which reflects the fact that women make up more than half the population as a whole.

We also know how hard it is for women to achieve real clout in the economic milieu. Women in management have been unable to penetrate the boardroom in significant numbers and the white male power brokers are still running things in corporate America.

For example, of the twelve thousand directorships of America's top companies, only about 5 percent are held by women. And those women who do reach senior management pay a severe personal price: 90 percent of male executives are married, but only 41 percent of female executives are; 28 percent of female executives have *never* been married. And women *still* are paid only 85 cents on the male compensation dollar.

There are other sour lemons being handed out to women. For example, society has not elected to be serious about parental leave. And for those who feel as Mr. and Mrs. Martin did in 1916, any benefits that a business has conceded is in danger of being taken away in tough economic times. Some of the larger companies, to their credit, have instituted changes, but when the economy goes sour, givebacks seem to be the order of the day. Corporations then think more about cost cutting than about innovative family-based programs. The result: advances have not significantly improved the lifestyle of the majority of working adults, especially women.

There also exists a kind of double standard that urges men to help their partners with family matters when it's convenient and socially correct, yet somehow still leaves the burden of housework and child care on the shoulders of the women. One has to look no further than TV ads to see that women are still being portrayed as the housebound homemaker, with dad slugging it out in the workplace.

In their research for *The Best Companies for Women*, Baila Zeitz and Lorraine Dusky found that even in the most enlightened workplaces, women are just beginning to penetrate the uppermost levels of senior management. The authors found that with the exception of five companies considered the very best, the inner management circle is virtually all white and male. It's obvious that the so-called glass ceiling we hear so much about isn't made up of glass at all, but of a thick, almost impenetrable layer of *men*.

And those women trying to make their way have heard, once too often, "Be patient. We'll promote you *next* year, dear." The men just don't understand why, after all these years, we who have families to support also, who have drive and skill and ambition, are no longer willing to accept promises that are never kept.

ENTREPRENEURIAL WOMEN

Women who have been frustrated by the length of time they have to wait in the foyer of the company boardroom are finding ways to express their ambition and creativity.

Some, like me, have joined a family business; others have started a business of their own.

William Dunkelberg, dean of the Temple University School of Business, has observed that the nature and structure of our economy are shifting from big companies to small, flexible, niche-oriented companies.

And why is that? Part of the answer is that small companies are getting a big boost from new technology. *Fortune* magazine a few years ago, in an article called "The Golden Age of Entrepreneurs," identified several factors that have made business ownership attractive to Americans of *both* genders: most notably, the article explains, is the big business power given to small companies by computers. When you can desktop-publish your own sales materials, send information instantly by modem to your representative in another city, and compute your profits in a nanosecond, then you're competitive in a big-time way.

Both men and women are starting new businesses every year, but women are doing it much more often . . . and more successfully. The 1980s saw women start companies at *five* times the rate of men.

At least 3.7 million of the 13 million sole proprietorships in the United States today are owned by women, nearly double the 1.9 million we owned ten years ago. And the U.S. Small Business Administration estimates that by the year 2000, the numbers of self-employed women will increase from one-quarter to one-half of all Americans owning their own businesses.

But even today, women in charge of their own businesses are becoming much more visible. *Working Woman* magazine, in a recent article saluting America's top women business owners, profiled some of the more conspicuous success stories. Included among the twenty-five were such well-known names as Jenny Craig and Carole Little and Donna Karan, women who run companies in fields of "traditional" women's interests—weight loss and clothing design. But also on the list were Dorothy Owen, chair of the Owen Steel Company and Helen Jo Witsell, CEO of Copeland Lumber Yards.

The trend seems clear: women want to take control of their lives in ways and industries previously closed to them. Some will start businesses with friends, some with family, and some will go to work for a family business that already exists.

And all of them should be prepared for at least the possibility of prejudice, just because they're women. Old habits die very hard. Renee Edelman, vice-president of the public relations firm founded by her father, Daniel, told me that "women have a much harder time in the business world. I don't think that it's easy for any of us. I don't care what business you're in," continued Edelman. "Not many women have resolved the conflict of what to do when you have a child. And what to do when you have two children. How do you balance all that with work?"

The late eighties demonstrated to women just how hard it was to "have it all," which had seemed an obtainable dream to many until they actually tried to fulfill the demands of a fast-track job as well as a home and children. There are, it turns out, no more superwomen than there are supermen. Women are going to have to try to sort out their priorities realistically.

Do Family Businesses Welcome Women?

Not every woman is fortunate enough to have the opportunity to join her family business, but what of those who do? Is it worth their while to give it a try or are they opening the door to yet more stress as they cope with family as well as business problems? Once again, it depends.

It depends on the personality and point of view of those in charge as well as the resolve of the daughter in question and the nature of the business. A daughter would have a very tough time working for a father who thinks that a woman ought to teach for a few years before doing something really important like marrying and settling down.

So, if you are a woman, one of your first tasks before joining mom or dad is to try to answer the question: "Does my family business welcome women?"

And then try to figure out on what that welcome depends . . .

- *It depends on whether the woman has siblings or not—especially brothers.* Fathers are much more likely to think of their daughters as possible successors if there are no sons available.
- *It depends on the credentials of the woman herself.* If she joins dad or mom after having been appointed VP of Sales for another company, her opinion is going to carry a lot more weight than if she's just completed her B.A. in business.
- *It depends on parental attitudes.* Do her parents now see her as an adult, with something real to offer the company because of her education and job training?
- *It depends on your partner's understanding of your commitment.* Does that person understand that sometimes the job will come first? And will that person actually help out with housework, child care, whatever is relevant in your life?

- *It depends on the strength of the woman.* She must be gutsy enough to make her own way, to figure things out for herself, and to fill in the educational gaps on her own. With the possible exception of daughters working for their much-admired mothers (they do exist, I interviewed about half a dozen), women will find a paucity of female role models in the workplace, whether they work for a family business or elsewhere.

LIFE CAN BE MORE REWARDING IN A FAMILY FIRM

My own experience has led me to believe that women are much more likely to make it to the boardroom working for the family business than they are in a nonfamily company, of which, according to a *Fortune* magazine study, a mere 1 percent are controlled by women.

In family firms, 24 percent have women as VP decision makers or higher. In most of my interviews, the women agreed that they had a better chance to fill a policy-making slot at the family firm than they would elsewhere. And for women in a family business, even the CEO position was not out of reach.

There are other potential pluses for women who are offered the opportunity to join their family's company:

- *You will have access to businesses generally closed to women.* Syms is a retail clothing company, which is a field that attracts a great many women. On the other hand, there are some daughters like Christine Procida. She is a project manager in her family's third-generation construction company, which also employs some of her brothers as project managers.

  How has she managed in this man's world? She told me: "You just go out there without a cocky attitude. I think if I

123

were to give anyone advice, I would say to just do your job and in time you'll start to gain respect."

- *You might get a better chance to do meaningful work.* Laboring for the greater good of the family, if you have a fulfilling relationship with them, can offer the kind of emotional satisfaction that would be hard to find in another corporate job.

- *You have a better chance at promotion in a family business.* Even if you're not in the running for the top job today, you will not be passed over just because you're a woman. After all, you're a daughter, or sister, or niece, to those guys running the show.

- Your financial rewards may be better. You may have stock in the company, and thus are personally interested in doing whatever has to be done to improve the company's value. Also, if you work for the kind of family business that promotes men and women alike, you will be getting a decent and fair salary for all those long hours.

- Your life might be easier if you're one of those women who is trying to have it all—family, children, and meaningful employment. Your children may be, after all, the grandchildren of the founder, who is going to want you home with them if they have strep throat. You're the link to the next generation —the eventual heirs.

- *You have the opportunity to arrange a more flexible work schedule.* My women respondents felt that they had received greater understanding from management during their childbearing years and a lot of freedom to deal with their family responsibilities. In general, the women I spoke with seemed reasonably contented with the corporate treatment they had received as they tried to juggle complicated lives.

- *You have a chance to invigorate your family's business with your feminine way of looking at things.* There are elements of your personality that you have developed just because you're a woman—your caring, your ability to listen with compassion, as well as the economically important truth that you understand 52 percent of the population and how and what they buy. Lillian Vernon, CEO of the $160 million mail-order company bearing her name, has said, "I know my customer because I *am* my customer."

The Relationship with Dad/Boss

Someone recently asked me, "What are you best known for?" and I answered, "For being Sy Syms' daughter." That's an answer that's okay for me to give now. I mean it, and I feel comfortable with it, but it wasn't always that way.

During the first few years working for my father, I was very sensitive about my actual contribution to the business and unsure about my worth to Syms and about my own identity.

My ego is stronger now, and I'm much more confident about what I have to offer the company. I'm lucky to have a father who also has a strong ego. He's not threatened by his child's accomplishments and strengths. I've heard enough horror stories from my interviewees to know that this can be a real problem in multigenerational companies.

Nevertheless, as good as our relationship was and is today, there were times in the beginning when I suffered from hellish insecurity and was sure that I had made a hideous mistake in thinking that I could offer the company anything—or get anything in return. I made a lot of wrong decisions as I learned the business, but I really think that it was during those dark days that I grew the most. And as time went on, I developed the nerve to take a really hard, analytical look at a mistake in judgment—that's when you can learn exponentially.

When you work for a parent, there is enormous potential for

pain. You want that person's admiration, and, especially at the beginning of a career, it's sometimes hard to come by. I'm lucky— I never could have developed the ability to look objectively at my faults without the great wealth of love and respect that I always received from my father, from the day I was born. That's a much more precious legacy to me than any fortune.

As we know, we are all, boys and girls, influenced by our parents from infancy. They are the central characters in the life of the very young child. It is also true that these same parents are the transmitters of culturally based attitudes on masculinity and femininity. It is from these early impressions that we learn what's okay to do.

It may be that the father has as much—or even more—impact on the developing child than the mother.

John Snarey, Ph.D., who is associate professor of ethics and human development at Emory University, was in charge of a research team that had tracked 248 men for forty years. They rated how these men related to their firstborn children, and then compared those findings with later behavior of those boys and girls.

The team discovered that daughters who were rated as being high achievers had fathers who were emotionally close to them during adolescence and who also were supportive of their daughters' athletic participation. The result: These girls learned "initiative, autonomy and how to interact with an adult male . . . crucial lessons for accomplishment in today's world."

Working with Mom the Founder

The pairs of CEO mothers and employee daughters I interviewed all seemed to enjoy close, fulfilling relationships—Kathryn Klinger and her mother, Georgette, who run their own skin care and cosmetics business; real estate coworkers Alice Mason and her daughter, Dominique Richard; Lynn Roberts and her mother, Dorothy, of

Echo Design Group; and Lynn Manulis, daughter of Martha Phillips, who founded New York City's elite shop Martha. All the daughters saw their mothers as admirable role models and caring mentors. The mothers were all proud of their daughters, and thrilled to have them working by their sides.

A typical comment came from Manulis: "I always thought that my mother was very glamorous. She is to this day, and is very charismatic. She is the kind of woman who when she walks into the room, you know she's there. Growing up, I always had the feeling that she was special. She always encouraged me. When she criticized me, she said, 'Please consider that it's because of my love for you.' Our honesty toward each other has always been a source of strength.

"She's also very intuitive. She reads people better than I do. She can't be pigeonholed or defined and I think she is a little bit larger than life. Because she has a tremendous amount of confidence, it's easy for her to allow the next person to be good, better, or best. . . . I think that we have a very unusual relationship. We're very good friends. I always felt that my mother and father were my champions."

Other daughters were also enthusiastic about their moms, and the mothers about their children — the families of produce distributor Frieda Caplan and Weight Watchers' Florine Mark come to mind. With so much mutual admiration being shared, it's no wonder that they all seem to work well together.

THE WOMAN EXECUTIVE: A HUMANIZING INFLUENCE

Because I think women do have greater opportunities available in their family businesses, I also think that family businesses may be among the first to learn to use women's strengths. Enough women are crawling up the managerial ladder for us to get an idea of these strengths that are the direct result of a woman's unique upbringing.

I think one thing that women in the workplace have learned recently is that it is not in their own self-interest to try to be anything other than their feminine selves. Those pinstriped days of wearing men's suiting and copying male aggressiveness are gone.

Women can give the workplace an additional and essential dimension by being encouraged to use our natural attributes. We have been trained to be excellent caretakers, to nurture, to support, to seek out the whole story, to want to know how families actually live. Although some women *do* want to grind an opponent's face in the dust, there are many who know how to build consensus, to cooperate toward a common goal, and who feel more comfortable operating that way.

Matilde Salganicoff, who is one of the outstanding research professionals studying women in family businesses, said in a recent issue of *Family Business Review* that "women order human experience by different priorities than men do." Salganicoff described the criteria by which women define themselves: their ability to care, the importance of love and sharing, the interrelationship of family and career, the ability to find alternatives in a work setting, perception of others' moods and feelings, the importance of the maternal role. Those criteria are juxtaposed with men's self-definitions, which usually center on personal autonomy and independence and the importance of success and achievement.

It seems clear that when a company learns to use a woman's strengths creatively, it can harness more easily the kind of team effort that most businesses try to foster for efficient management.

Toward Being Taken Seriously

Nearly every expert reports that most family business owners will choose daughters as a last resort or by default. A University of Montana study of fifty-nine family-operated businesses found that most fathers would rather pass their companies to a nonrelative than to a daughter. Paul C. Rosenblatt, a professor of family social sciences who conducted the study, said, "Daughters were almost never considered seriously as people who could take over."

But customs must change, because of the realities of society. The divorce rate has been hovering at about 50 percent for nearly a decade now, and daughters—perhaps by default—are being taken much more seriously as possible inheritors of the business.

Even with their new prominence in management positions, many daughters have found real acceptance sticky going—both within the company and with clients.

Rhona Weinberg Gewelber had no intention of going into her family's grain and dairy business, which was about to pass on to the third generation. Her father, Bob Weinberg, was the son of the founder of this $100-million-a-year West Coast company. She saw the business as "men's work" and wanted no part of it. What she wanted was to work in a field in which she could use her bachelor's degree in religion and philosophy. Fortunately, she had an older brother.

But the older brother was not stimulated by the grain business either, and followed his own interest in medicine, entering medical school and specializing in pediatrics. In desperation, the father turned to his daughter and asked her to join the company. By this time, Rhona Weinberg had some experience in the real workplace and realized that jobs combining religion and philosophy were not readily available. Tired of uninteresting sales and secretarial jobs, Rhona Weinberg joined the family firm. It turned out to be a good fit and today she is vice president of marketing and the new heir apparent.

But a woman in a managerial position sometimes does not really know if she is being taken seriously—especially if she enters what was previously a man's world.

A recent issue of *Family Business* magazine published an article by David M. Marson, owner—with his brother, Richard—of the Newcan company of Holbrook, Massachusetts, a manufacturer of perforated metal tubes and components for the filter industry.

In the article, David Marson talked about how he had wanted his daughter, Marsha, to join the company, although she was trained as a CPA and was not especially anxious to change fields. But the other possible beneficiaries were not interested. Marson admitted that it would be wonderful "to have continuity of management, to know after a century the company would still be producing benefits and employment for the family."

Marsha Marson did enter the business as the heir apparent. At first, she not only didn't know if it was working, her father didn't either.

Said David Marson: "The transition from public accounting to manufacturing was not difficult, but there was a culture change that amazed Marsha even though I had, in my preliminary letter, detailed the type of people she would come in contact with in the factory. She encountered uneducated people with openly expressed prejudices, the lack of a work ethic, inconsistent performances even from highly compensated foremen. Deliberately introducing one's daughter into such an environment is not terribly comforting.

"It didn't help my morale when I observed some uncomplimentary writing about her on the men's room wall. Rather than become angry I concluded the person who wrote it was stupid, but for a father the incident was disquieting."

Eventually, all parties became used to each other and settled down, and Marsha was put in charge of the plant's production-control planning—a successful appointment.

But David Marson admitted that the transition would have been easier if Marsha had been a man: "There would have been fewer barriers to break down, fewer precedents to establish. It would have been easier on me, and I would not have had as many concerns about the present and the future. . . . Those concerns were based not on doubts about her ability, but on emotional elements between fathers and daughters."

The very idea of daughters running a company is new, and can often be in conflict with family myth and custom. Traditionally, the heir is the oldest son. And until very recently if the daughter had any connection with the business she would marry well in order to bring a trusted and faithful son-in-law into the family business. I remember hearing conversations while I was growing up about whom I was going to marry. I already knew that he was supposed to be a good hard-working addition to Dad's business.

Although I think that I managed to forge my own identity over the years, I received an awful lot of messages about the traditional roles that I was expected to play. Custom is hard to overcome. The going is tough for an ambitious woman, and we should have no illusions about it.

But chinks in the armor of masculine solidarity do appear, especially if there are no suitable sons around.

A recent issue of the *Cincinnati Enquirer* profiled a young woman named Katie Brown. Just twenty-six years old, she had been named heir presumptive by her father, Mike Brown, who happens to be general manager of the Bengals, Cincinnati's NFL football franchise.

Talk about a business that wouldn't be expected to consider including a woman in any capacity except cheerleader, much less future general manager. Of course, Katie Brown has never played professional football, and is currently the organization's corporate secretary and legal counsel. Would she ever become involved in choosing players? Mike Brown, her father, whose own football career was limited to quarterbacking for Dartmouth in the 1950s, was quoted by the *Enquirer* as saying, "When we get to the draft this year, she'll sit in and be welcomed and have a say if she wants it.

"We'll just see how it evolves from there, but she very well could have a big role in those decisions down the road. There are plenty of men making those kinds of decisions now who don't have big-time experience as a player or coach, including myself."

I see this as an example of family businesses leading the way into uncharted waters. Women often are given a real chance by their parents, and if they succeed, the door opens a little wider for all of us.

Daddy's Little Girl

If you don't want to be treated in business like Daddy's little girl, you're going to have to fight a lot of dragons. You fight with a new behavior that works, and you take great pains to avoid favoritism of any kind.

Marla Schaeffer works for Claire's Stores, Inc., one of the country's largest dealers in accessories, and founded by her dad. Marla Schaeffer described to me her experience: "I always had a struggle working for my father. I always wanted to go off and prove myself somewhere else. My father's attitude about me working for him was, you're working for me because you can't do anything else. I'm going to take care of you.

"My father is a caretaker. He loves to take care of people. He always made it easy on me. If I wanted to get a job someplace else, it was always 'Why would you want to do that when you can work for me? I'm going to pay you double what you might make any-place else.' He's always sweetened the deal."

Marla Schaeffer found behavior that worked for her, and it didn't include acting like Daddy's little girl. When I asked her what advice she had for people who want to go into the family business, Marla told me that "you must have a good sense of yourself going into the job. Never put yourself in a position where your father can say, 'If it weren't for me . . .' That's a very terrible place to be."

Nancy Lampton's story illustrates how hard it is for fathers to really let their daughters grow up. She is the chairman and CEO of the American Life and Accident Insurance Company of Kentucky, a business founded by her grandfather, and of which her father, Dinwiddie Lampton, Jr., is president. He is a southern gentleman of the old school and proudly declares himself an "evolving chauvinist."

In a TV interview a few years ago, Mr. Lampton said that he found it very hard to make the leap from regarding his daughter as his little girl to viewing her as a capable businesswoman. And that daughter, with twenty-two years' experience working alongside her father, accepts part of the responsibility for his attitude: "We weren't serious, capable businesswomen in the beginning. The training came through work."

Parents are usually protective of their children, and sometimes no matter how hard the daughter tries to grow up, and fight her own battles, Dad can't help but mix in.

Fathers sometimes do their daughters a disservice when they rescue them from predicaments again and again. These also may be situations in which a son would have been left to manage by himself—"to learn to be a man." Fathers might think that they're offering their daughters love and protection, but the fundamental message is one of "no confidence." Women in business need more than equal opportunity to make safe decisions—they need the opportunity to get out there and learn to take care of themselves when the hard ones come up.

The Lord Helps Those . . .

It's up to you to convince your parents and coworkers that you're a grownup and can fill a much more important role than symbol of the next generation. You want to have a real job, and real authority, and make a useful contribution to the family business. But how can you ensure that the older generation is ever going to take you seriously—ever going to let you appear in your real guise as adult?

I recently answered a question on this topic in my advice column for *Family Business* magazine. A reader asked me, "As a daughter, how do you avoid being treated like Daddy's little girl?"

I hope the guidelines that I shared with my magazine readers will be of help to you.

1. Don't ever ask for special treatment. You're just like any other employee, no better, and certainly not entitled to favors.
2. If you work for your father directly, be open. Communicate. You can be supportive, but you also have to tell him the bad news.
3. Don't be the bearer of tales or requests from other employees. It is not your responsibility to carry to your father any information that is not related to your job.
4. Tell your father at once—in private—if he treats you unprofessionally in front of coworkers.
5. Leave your mother out of it. If it's not your job to intercede with your father on another worker's behalf, it's not your mother's to speak to your father for you. Don't establish a behavioral triangle—it's counterproductive.

6. Most importantly: Be professional. If you don't want to be perceived as Daddy's little girl, don't act like it. No crying, no whining, no complaining, no cute behavior. You're in the real world, even if some of the players are your nearest relatives.

I've been asked whether I see myself first as a woman or as a company president. My answer is that I am a woman president, with all its benefits and obligations and uncertainties. I have worked for Syms long enough now to have a firm grasp of the skills I need for filling my responsibility and all things considered, the pluses outweigh the minuses. I do think that as long as women managers continue to learn to be more effective, and as long as they are willing to give their sisters in the workforce a boost from time to time, and to serve as role models for those women coming up through the ranks, then perhaps we have a chance someday to be treated as true colleagues in the boardroom and as equal partners with men, and participate fully in the economic decision making that affects all our lives.

Chapter

7

Relationships Within the Nuclear Family

A friend loves you for your intelligence, a mistress for your charm,
but your family's love is unreasoning; you were born into it and are
of its flesh and blood. Nevertheless it can irritate you more than any
group of people in the world.

André Maurois, *The Art of Living*

When you join a family business, you get to work with people who know you well, whom you can trust, and who will look out for your best interest in addition to their own. But it also is true that when you work with your relatives—whether siblings or those farther afield—you may bring to your worklife all those sticky family issues that made you want to leave home when you were an adolescent.

Families and businesses are different. The business's main goal is to turn a profit so that it can expand and grow. From the point of view of the longevity of the family business, I believe that the familiar slogan is largely true: "The family that makes money together stays together." That's basic, and so if the family firm is to survive, business must come first. It has to make money, or it will cease to be a business.

The family's goal, on the other hand, is to develop a nurturing support structure for its members . . . and also to train those members eventually to leave the nest.

In addition, there are other obvious differences between the two systems:

- Emotion may rule the family system, but practicality rules the business system.
- A family nurtures and makes allowances for individual differences, but a business is interested in molding you into a team member capable of producing its goods or services efficiently and profitably.
- A family will do almost anything to resist change, but a business must learn to take advantage of change to remain competitive.

The Opposing Systems and Conflict

Change always occurs—both in business matters and human relationships. The difference in reaction to predictable change is basic to family and business systems, and one of the reasons why they are hard to integrate successfully.

These two systems can move in opposing directions, and, like the layers of the earth, when they move they cause friction. The result can be an earthquake. For example, it is almost certain that if you work in a family business that employs several members with varying and sometimes opposing interests, sooner or later there is going to be:

1. *Conflicting attitudes about money.*

Each family member will have his or her personal agenda, and there is no reason to assume that the good of the family business will always come first. Your relatives might not even agree on what the good of the family business is. Some members might want larger dividends now, others will want to invest some or all of their dividends to build a larger, stronger company, and there will be some who might want to sell all or part of the company to an outside buyer.

Within the family, there may be resentments on the part of some who feel that they or their children were slighted when the corporate pie was divided. Their agenda is redressing the perceived inequity. You could have as many potential financial agendas as you have relatives.

A time-tested guideline: Remember the goose and the golden eggs—do not kill the goose. The financial well-being of the company should come first. If you and your relatives cannot agree on what that is, you have the makings of a self-destructive business issue. Get help. There are plenty of competent business and financial consultants who make their living offering solutions —not only on money matters, but on a whole range of business and personal problems that could come up as your family business develops and grows.

How to find the correct consultant? If you had been looking for a family business "doctor" a decade ago, you might have had to settle for your lawyer or accountant; usually, neither one was trained to deal with interpersonal issues.

But today you have plenty of places to look for help. You could start with the Family Firm Institute, in Brookline, Massachusetts, which has 680 member consultants. Or perhaps your trade association can put you in touch with business owners in your area who have had similar problems and have worked with professional advisers. As always, personal referrals from people whose opinion you trust is the most reliable guide.

Probably the most important factor in deciding whom to hire is "personal chemistry"—in addition to, of course, appropriate credentials and references.

A few things to look for:

- Do you think the prospective consultant shows empathy for your family problems? Does he or she seem to understand what you're all about?
- Is he or she able to offer an organized, problem-solving plan once you've identified the problems? Basically, does the potential consultant seem sharp, knowledgeable, and up-to-date?
- Is the consultant accessible? Available to answer questions as they come up?
- Does this person share your family business's values and does he or she understand your goals? In other words, is this consultant on your family's wave length?

2. *Jockeying for power positions within one generation.*

You might suffer from a serious case of childhood sibling rivalry, which you've never laid to rest and which has followed you into the workplace. Or the children of two founding brothers —close cousins but not friends—might disagree about the next person to fill the presidential slot.

A guideline: Whoever is in charge of the company must be absolutely clear about who does what and when a family member might expect to move ahead. In this case, the founding brothers ought to agree between themselves about the composition of future top management and their decision should be clearly spelled out with no ambiguity.

3. *A challenge to the authority of the founding or managing generation.*

Eventually, the Young Turks are going to want to take over. At least the potential heirs in our society—unlike ancient Rome—don't usually murder all close relatives to effectively eliminate competition, but emotional chaos can be extremely enervating for all concerned and should be avoided at all costs.

When I first started working at Syms full time in 1978, I saw Sy as the all-powerful founder. He had an active and curious mind and always knew how to figure out the best solution to a problem.

As time went on and we worked together closely, I realized that as much as I loved and admired my father, I occasionally disagreed with him. In general, I tend to be more impatient. We're both looking into the same tunnel, but he's looking back into the tunnel, and I'm looking forward. I am of a different generation, after all, and my perspective cannot possibly always be his. This was, and is, a terrible source of conflict for me.

But at the basis of our relationship is trust. Sy trusts my judgment and I think that he's one of the best retailers in the country. With mutual admiration in place, we let our working relationship develop from there. Sy does have an autocratic management style, and has jokingly called himself "the dictator." I know that if I feel strongly about a particular change, and Sy does not agree, I just have to prove my point over time. Even though our objectives—the growth and well-being of the company—are the same, he is, after all, the boss and the majority shareholder. He's entitled to make the final decision.

A guideline: Both the managing and upcoming generations must compromise. They have to talk to each other about day-to-day processes and future goals. Sy has told me that he thinks I have taught him to communicate better. I think I have, too, and consider that to be one of my successes at Syms.

I truly believe that the new generation has to demonstrate patience. It is not productive, it's rarely smart, and it's never polite to try to force out the founder/parent just because you think you can do it better. Of course you think you can do it better, but if you cannot wait your turn, be creative and become a founder/entrepreneur elsewhere.

4. *Controversy over what is perceived as unequal and unfair compensation.*

This argument could arise with either working family members or nonworking family members, any of whom might think that they were being shortchanged in some way.

I remember a letter written to me last year in my role as advice columnist for *Family Business* magazine. My reader shared the following problem with me:

"I am a woman in a family business with four brothers . . . Like two of my older brothers, I am a project manager.

"My problem is compensation. I am not married and have no children. I do the same work as my brothers, but only make about 40 percent of what they do. When I discuss this with my father, he says it's because my brothers have to support wives and children. This makes me so angry I want to quit. How can I get my father to see this issue from my point of view?"

She was right to be angry. As I said in my answer to her, "What you want is simply equal pay for equal work: You are entitled to this not as a favor but because it's *the law.*"

A great deal of trouble can be avoided by actually writing down the company's compensation policy.

Are all family members in one age group paid the same salary? Or is financial equality limited to dividends, with salaries awarded strictly on the basis of performance?

Is there a company policy of taking care of all family members? Is there a sensible division between voting stock and nonvoting stock? And what rights have those holders of nonvoting stock? If all these questions are thought through by the financial managers, and actually expressed in a family business manifesto, then everyone should know where he or she stands and what to expect in the future.

5. *The issue of family conflict resolution.*

There has to be some framework in place before conflict arises —as it inevitably does. Disagreement, rivalry, personality clashes are going to happen at some time or another among family members.

A guideline: The solution for this problem, too, rests with the generation in charge. It is up to them to be sure that techniques exist to talk things out within the family, and if this fails, to require that the protagonists submit to an outside arbiter.

Tried-and-true techniques for conflict resolution before you need to introduce an outside facilitator include:

Family meetings. These could be spur-of-the-moment, or regularly scheduled. It's most important that disagreements be aired in an open atmosphere.

Family retreats. Everyone involved goes to a tranquil spot to escape the distractions of the business. A change of scene can sometimes lead to a change in thinking and new perspectives applied to old problems.

Family councils. Family business consultant Dennis T. Jaffe, writing in his book *Working With the Ones You Love*, defined a family council as "the organizational and strategic planning arm of a family, where all members meet to decide values, policy, and direction." Every relevant family member ought to participate.

One of the primary purposes of family councils is to eliminate secrecy in management: it's not true that problems disappear if they're ignored. They fester and cause greater resentment later on.

Jaffe pointed out that the council is useful for developing and implementing three types of planning: (1) individual plans, which concentrate on personal goals; (2) family plans, which determine the overall goals of the family and discuss what resources are needed to implement the goals; and (3) business plans, which involve such topics as control of the company, family involvement in management, and direction of the business.

Participants in a series of family councils might not agree with everything that is said, but at least they are well informed about the direction of the company and their place in its future.

Workable Guidelines

When I first started to interview members of family businesses for this book, I was hoping that universal guidelines which spelled success would pop out at me. I knew which family relationships I wanted to explore. I wanted to see what, if anything, was lacking within my own family, so I was especially interested in families that were like my own in some way. I was the daughter of a male CEO, I was the oldest, and I had both brothers and sisters, some of whom were interested in working for the company.

Most of my interviewees were employed by their parents, and many worked alongside siblings. I heard very little about other relatives.

There weren't too many families among my sample of forty-four like that of Florine Mark, for example, who started a successful Weight Watchers franchise in Detroit some years ago. She owns the business with one of her sisters, and in addition has had various combinations of her five children work for her from time to time, as well as another sister, a brother-in-law, her parents, and a son-in-law. The upcoming generation of grandchildren is still too young to think about employing them, but the Mark family intends to continue to include all comers.

I found that this arrangement was an exception. My sampling suggests that by the time my generation achieves management status, the founding generation has consolidated power—leaving perhaps one sibling alone at the top. Other relatives over time seem to disappear from family businesses—perhaps they've gone off to start their own family firms.

There were two issues that surfaced as universal to a family business experience with members of a nuclear family.

The first: forging a unique identity while being part of the family team in the workplace. This involves psychic separation from parents and other family members and a desire for recognition of one's contributions to the company.

Dominique Richard, daughter of Alice Mason, one of New York City's top real estate brokers, who deals mostly in multi-million-dollar properties, admires her mother's style and talent, but found following in her footsteps somewhat daunting.

"At first, it wasn't easy for me," Dominique Richard told me. "I think she thought that because she had started from nothing, and everything was ready-made for me, that it would be easy. But when you're involved in something new, you don't think like that. You think it's difficult.

"After a while the ladies in the office got a little more mellow, and understood more of what I was trying to do. And I started to make a few deals, so it kind of worked into itself. But it took me a while."

The second theme concerns dealing with conflict: the mechanisms and systems that have been created for conflict resolution, and the preventive maintenance that we at Syms call "damage control."

The effectiveness of family talent in putting out emotional fires and convincing all concerned to share common goals is the single most important aspect in keeping a family business humming along.

Siblings: Your Best Support System?
Although there are many benefits to working for a family business, the potential for serious trouble is always lurking. It's just not realistic to assume that because you're "family," you're all going to get along as if you were living an episode of a pleasant 1950s TV sitcom.

Unless every member of your immediate family has received equal and sufficient doses of attention, love, support, and encouragement, which is pretty unlikely, the chances are good that you've arrived at adulthood with a whole trunk of resentments against every single one of your nearest and dearest.

Could the residue of some childhood slight pop up inappropriately in an office situation?

Could a sociopathic brother working across the hall from you find pleasure in disrupting harmony at every turn?

Could your sister, the holder of voting stock but up to now supposedly happy in her career as a city planner, suddenly decide that you are not an effective CEO and that she'd like a shot at the job herself?

These things could happen, and you can bet that sooner or later they will unless you are on your guard and ready to put techniques of conflict management into play.

Even if you've gotten along pretty well with your siblings over the years, once you're all out in the real world, disagreements take on a new urgency, and new criteria apply. You now have your career to think about.

Whatever stormy history you and your sibling may have together, this is a person whom you want to be a good friend, not a competitor. I remember reading about a psychological study a few years ago in *The New York Times* that demonstrated good relationships with siblings significantly enhanced the mental health of those involved.

Other psychologists have come to similar conclusions. Dr. Stephen Bank, a Connecticut psychologist who also teaches at Wesleyan, has written that an only child frequently feels deprived when he or she reaches adulthood and understands better what it's like to have siblings.

"It's nice to have someone who shared memories with you," wrote Dr. Bank in *The Sibling Bond*. "And unless an only child went out and adopted a good buddy, a friend, as a sibling, there is no one to remember with once the leaves start falling from the trees."

I think we have to accept the fact that siblings are important to us, emotionally and as allies in the business. Family business success can depend on your alliance with a brother or sister.

You have a lot in common: you grew up in the same house, you share values and goals—and usually parents, one hopes that you love and trust each other. These bonds ought to be strong enough to forge a formidable partnership. How do you keep them from breaking?

Family business consultants John L. Ward and Craig E. Aronoff, writing in a recent issue of *Nation's Business*, can help us with a checklist. Their advice:

1. If you have a gripe, talk about it in private. No screaming in the office. Don't speak to your sibling in a way that you wouldn't like. Don't talk about your sibling behind his or her back.

2. Don't bad-mouth your sibling to your spouse. Why should your spouse hear nothing but negatives about your sibling? Is it any wonder that your wife can't stand your brother? You've been presenting him as a villain for years.

3. Don't evaluate or judge your sibling. Engage in a little self-criticism first.

4. Don't poach in your brother's or sister's territory. You have a job of your own; leave theirs alone. Give them plenty of room to make decisions.

5. Try to have a cordial social relationship with your siblings. If you spend time together, it can deepen your relationship, and if you make certain that you all talk openly, misunderstandings will not arise.

6. Unless there are pressing reasons to run the company by autocratic rule, those involved should govern by consensus. It makes for a stronger management team and will keep family business members happy.

7. In the business setting, be sure you put the needs of the business first. You're all adults now and surely can divorce personal problems from management decisions.

8. Communicate and compromise. Give-and-take among siblings is possible . . . and necessary if the upcoming management generation is to run the family business rationally and profitably.

A story of compromise between brothers that worked—eventually—is told by psychiatrist Roy Menninger, president of the Menninger Foundation in Topeka.

The Menninger family firm, a psychiatric hospital, was founded in 1925. Forty years after the company had been established, was successful, and had passed to the founder's two sons, the nonfamily professionals in the clinic decided that the then president—the

148

older brother, Roy's uncle Karl—was "much too totalitarian, much too arbitrary, and much too focused on himself as the only source of wisdom."

As the hospital was a collegial organization, it was felt that the professionals needed greater autonomy and would prefer someone more flexible at the helm. The younger brother, William, was given the task of asking Karl to reduce his responsibilities. He is said to have responded, "Reduce? Hell! I'll quit!" And he did. He insisted for the rest of his life that he'd been fired. Within eighteen months, the younger brother died of cancer and his oldest son, Roy, was elected to the presidency. Roy describes how the wheels were set in motion for history to repeat itself:

"Can you imagine the setting? Here were these two giants who were gone and I, somebody whose name happened to be Menninger, had come in to take their place. I had never run anything. I was no manager and I didn't know anything about being an executive. I was a kindly psychiatrist, a little like my father. For ten years I struggled and kept ahead of the troops by learning faster than they did. It was working very well.

"But I had one problem—a brother, Walter. I was afraid that we would relive the family history and get into a terrible power struggle. My brother is very bright, very quick, very assertive, and has no problems at all in telling you what he thinks. As the older brother, I always looked over my shoulder, wondering if the younger brother would overtake me.

"So, in what I considered a very rational way, I persuaded Walter to become director of the state hospital three miles down the road. In effect, I exiled him. He accepted this, but before he left, he said to me, 'Roy, I'm going to do better than you at everything I can.'

"Walt did a very effective job down the road. And then there came a time when I just had to have a chief of staff. I could no longer run the company by myself. We created a search committee. Its task was to examine potential candidates, which is what they did for eighteen months. Finally, I heard from them: 'Roy, we have talked to people from other states and other countries and have interviewed quite a number. We've found the only person we think is qualified. He happens to be your brother.' "

The story has a satisfactory ending. The two brothers compromised—each taking on responsibilities in nonoverlapping areas. By governing separate realms, they've managed to work together efficiently.

Psychology Is More than Blaming Your Parents

We're more than what we eat. We're what we feel, and how we react to people, and how we express ourselves. And although it would be simplistic to say that what we are is a direct result of our childhood, it would be foolish to say that it has nothing to do with it.

Our parents' relationship to each other and to us is fundamental to our development. From infancy, we pick up cues praising accepted behaviors and condemning others. Unless the family is wildly dysfunctional, the desire of most children is to please authority figures—thus, the twig gets bent into a certain shape specific to your family, and you behave in a way approved of by your clan.

If you have several brothers and sisters, you will each compete for the approval of your parents. There are those children who please easily, and those who never can no matter how hard they try —these emotional successes and failures are likely to follow the child into young adulthood, influencing their personalities, behaviors, and how the outside world reacts to them.

If a person has had an unhappy childhood, it is perfectly possible for him or her to become a contented, productive adult. People like this most likely will have to remove themselves from the influence of their nuclear family. If this describes you, you are not an appropriate candidate for the family business. It would be just plain stupid, for instance, for a younger brother to follow his much-disliked older brother into a work situation in which he would have to compete with him constantly.

Most families learn from their difficulties, and most siblings manage a way of interacting with each other and their parents that can be satisfying and supportive.

I certainly know from my own experience that family relationships do not change magically once the whole cast is assembled in the workplace. It's important for those of us in family businesses to try to figure out our relationships because we face them every day —and they affect our careers and success. If we do nothing to try to understand why we act the way we do, then our interactions are going to remain difficult and we will make no progress toward personal happiness. We will remain victims of the consequences of denying problems within the family firm.

Patterns of Family Relationships

Many psychologists have attempted to categorize family relationships, and some have constructed descriptive patterns in order to classify these relationships.

I was especially interested in Dr. Michael E. Kerr's discussion of interlocking relationships within families in *Handbook of Family Therapy* (Brunner/Mazel, 1981) because I think it applies to most families. Dr. Kerr uses the triangle as a device to illustrate basic relationships. It's not hard to figure out: in most families, the couple is the basic unit. Then kids are born, and there are three, and then possibly more.

According to Dr. Kerr, most family dynamics can be explained through the use of sets of interlocking triangles. Triangles show the ebb and flow of emotional interaction: usually, of the three people in a triangle, two are insiders and one an outsider, although that can change at any moment.

For example, "If a mother directs her relationship interests towards one of her children, the father can feel the relief of not having to deal with his wife's anxiety about him and not having to confront potential emotional issues in their marital relationship. On the other hand, the mother's emotional overinvestment in the child may leave the father feeling rejected and uncomfortable. In this case, he will make moves to restore the marital togetherness."

Additional triangles may be conceived for any family relationship: brother-brother-father; mother-daughter-brother; and so forth. I find diagramming problematic relationships useful, sometimes, in helping me to step back from a situation and achieve a little distance. For a little while, I can be the objective outsider.

I think making use of any model that fits your situation is fine if it helps you order your thoughts when there are too many issues involved to see the main one clearly. If drawing triangles, or making charts, or applying another system of analysis gives a name to your situation and makes you realize that a lot of others have had a problem with this, too—and it helps you to work the problem through—then it's worth doing.

I know that I learned management and caretaking skills growing up. The oldest of six children, especially if the child is a girl, has to; it's expected of her by everyone.

Some writers interested in families have suggested that birth order has a great deal to do with how we see ourselves as well as how we view the world.

Clinical psychologist Walter Toman was the researcher who

delved deepest, and first, into the subject of the influence of sibling position on personality and behavior. He was one of the earliest to suggest that certain patterns of behavior developed by children in families was the direct result of their position in the birth order.

I think there's something to this: I was struck, for example, by the preponderance of firstborns among the CEOs whom I interviewed—not 100 percent, certainly, but a majority, especially among the women leaders. And oldest children, researchers agree, expect to be in charge—it's their natural role.

Dr. Kevin Leman, writing in *The Birth Order Book: Why You Are the Way You Are*, lists the following traits typical of firstborns: perfectionistic, reliable, conscientious, list maker, well organized, critical, serious, scholarly. Firstborns seem very highly motivated to achieve and are usually very disciplined—good traits for a company president.

This, of course, does not mean that children elsewhere in the birth order cannot achieve high position—it doesn't even mean that they necessarily fit the average profile that applies to their place in the birth order.

Dr. Leman describes the middle child as being the perfect mediator: this child tries hard to avoid conflict, shows loyalty to his or her peer group, and has many friends. This is also the child with the fewest pictures in the family photo album. But every middle child is not a mediator, nor does he or she always avoid conflict.

And the youngest child? Traditionally, this person is charming, precocious, manipulative, and not very reliable. But, here again, not every youngest is a feckless charmer and showoff who would make a super salesperson.

Only children are less prepared to deal with peer-level social interaction than children with siblings. They are, naturally enough, comfortable with adults and usually independent in thought and behavior. These are not pack animals and frequently have a good sense of self, having spent years absorbing the undiluted admiration of their parents.

Although these are only stereotypes, based on average statistics, there is enough truth to these profiles for us to at least consider them when we try to figure out what makes each of us tick.

I've learned something about family relationships by living in a family, as well as by being married, by reading, talking with people, undergoing therapy, and having a relationship with a family mentor as well as an outside business mentor: a bad situation, whether within a family, a business, or a family business, *can* get better.

Today, four of Sy Syms' children work within the company, and we all see ourselves as part of the management team. I think the comment of my brother Stephen—the oldest male child—says it for all of us: "As for overcoming my wounds as the passed-over oldest son, I healed them by getting more involved in what I'm doing in the company, looking at the larger scope of things. Fortunately, it's a growing company and there's plenty of room for everyone to feel important regardless of titles."

The Delicate Balance of Conflict Management

When considering conflict management, I like to stress the part that balance plays in any resolution. You have to balance everyone's needs as best you can, and must use tact and fairness in dealing with all family members. But I think that it's possible to learn by doing.

I love an apt quote reported by management consultant Leslie Dashew Isaacs in a 1989 issue of *Insight*. "The Chinese have a wonderful way of looking at 'crisis,' " reported Isaacs. "Their symbol for this concept includes one character signifying 'danger,' another signifying 'opportunity.' The challenges or dangers of working with one's family are great: and so are the opportunities and payoffs. With careful attention to all three systems [family, business, personal lives] and reverence for the delicate balance one must maintain, families can work miracles together."

I agree. I think you just have to remember to stay focused on these simple points when you make management decisions.

- *Clarity of purpose.* Everyone should clearly understand their rights and responsibilities within the company.
- *Compromise.* Both between and within generations.
- *Commitment to the same goals.* Corporate culture themes and business goals should be spelled out.
- *Communication.* Talk, and then talk some more.
- *Creativity.* Don't use the same old models. Experiment with new ones that more accurately reflect the unique needs of your family.

All these are easy to talk about, but hard to do. I steadfastly believe that if you have trouble implementing any of the above, consider the alternatives and find outside facilitators who can help get you back on track. The next generation expects it of you.

Steve Karol, who runs HMK Group Companies, a diversified corporation with interests in steel, railroads, and office furniture, with several of his siblings, talked to me about how his family business manages conflict. When Steve and his brothers disagree, "instead of having a consultant come in every time we have an argument, we set up an internal system of feedback that we use periodically just to air out everything. One of the biggest problems families have is this thing we call 'gunny sacking.' You've got a sack on your back and every time you get mad you throw a problem into the sack and don't say anything. It doesn't go away. Pretty soon the sack gets real heavy and either you're going to have to dump it or you're going to get crushed by it. Most people dump it. But how do you dump it? By exploding.

"You can always tell when someone's sack is getting heavy— they get irritable. When we see that happening, we call a feedback session. My sister will be the facilitator because she's trained in psychology, and my mother and two brothers will sit in and we'll talk."

The moral: Don't let bad feelings and irritations pile up. The eventual eruption is never constructive. Empty your sack by talking about it—using whatever method your family has put in place.

Chapter

8

What About Mom?

With very few exceptions, while her husband is still alive the wife usually doesn't fit in the family business—not in a salaried way, with a real title, unless she's in partnership with her spouse. Of the businesses in my survey that started out that way, only two remained mom-and-pop for more than one generation: the third-generation Woods family of Sylvia's Restaurant in New York City and the fifth-generation Voses of Vose Galleries in Boston. The Vose family, currently run by twin brothers Bill and Terry, was the only one in my group in which two generations of wives worked together—indeed, was one of the very few companies in which *any* of the wives were included.

Herbert Russell, head of H. J. Russell and Company, an Atlanta-based construction firm, expressed the sentiments of many a founder/entrepreneur's wife: "She wouldn't work here if we paid her a billion dollars a day. She runs the house. I know who the chief is once I enter it." And although the wife of *Black Enterprise* founder Earl Graves works in his publishing business on a daily basis and draws a salary, she keeps a low profile and plays mostly a supportive role.

As for titles, if wives and/or mothers do have them, they are more or less meaningless. Koke Cummins, president of Mansfield Industries, was very forthright: "My wife is the director or assistant secretary or secretary. The fact that I can't tell you for sure means she's not really involved at all. Basically, it's just a title. She has very little involvement other than what she hears from me when I come home at night."

Mrs. Cummins, a psychotherapist who specializes in family counseling, is described by her son Bruce as service giver and family nurturer: "My father is a very analytical, left-brain person. My mother couldn't tell you what twelve times eleven is, but she can look at me and say, 'You're sighing just like your dad. What does it mean?' Now, I wasn't sighing in order to generate an inquiry, I was sighing because that's how I relieve stress, but my mother can read people very well. She is kind of the center that holds things together. I don't mean that things would fall apart without her, but I think her objectivity can mean a lot to a couple of analytical, number-crunching businessmen."

Many wives show talent in arranging the social life important to the family business, which is an area that doesn't generate bottom-line income directly but which family members agree can be invaluable.

Renée Edelman, a company vice-president, describes her mother's role in Edelman Public Relations: "My mother played a big role in entertaining clients at a moment's notice, giving parties, really leading the way for my father in a social context in Chicago, getting him on a par with CEOs. Their names were in the society pages, and although my father says that referrals came through his business, I think my mother was a big help, too, and that they were a team that worked hard together. She was my father's right arm, although I don't know whether he'll admit it."

It is not surprising that many of these family-business wives would begin to doubt their self-worth, when year after year of behind-the-scenes helping never showed on the balance sheet. Although most of these wives didn't ever join their husbands' businesses, some did become entrepreneurs themselves.

Elizabeth Durkin, who works in the family law firm, has a mother who is an inspiration to her daughter: raising seven children took several decades, but as she worked as a full-time home-maker, she always took classes, and graduated from college the same year that Elizabeth graduated from high school. Eight years ago, her mother opened an Irish imports store. Elizabeth Durkin says admiringly of her mom: "She always said she'd rather be worn out than left out!"

THE BUSINESS AS MISTRESS

The family portrayed in the TV series *Father Knows Best* might have seemed ideal to some of our parents' generation, but the reality of the husbandly breadwinner was often less palatable. The founder/entrepreneur probably was not available to hear all about the school problems of his adorable tykes, but was on the road, or working late, or entertaining a client. And a lot of wives found themselves totally responsible for all matters relating to home and family.

Curtis L. Carlson, founder of the Carlson Companies, the travel, hotel, and marketing megacorp, understands all about the demands made by success:

"If you want to be an entrepreneur, that means you eat, drink, and sleep your business, and that the most important thing is business, and the part of a wife is to take care of the children and not cause her husband to have to fight dragons all day long and then go home and fight dragons all over again."

Indeed, many a neglected wife will see her husband's involvement in the company as destructive but will feel powerless to change her spouse's behavior.

Psychiatrist Roy Menninger described a relevant case history at a family business conference:

"Often I see in families who come into therapy that the two children are fighting considerably and the issue appears on the surface to be 'What's wrong with these two kids?' What often emerges in the course of family therapy is that the kids are playing out an issue that is going on between the mother and the father.

"The fight is really between the parents, but the parents deny and suppress that. They do everything to hide that information, and keep talking instead about the kids. But it's *their* problem.

"This kind of pattern occurs often in families where a wife marries a man who has really taken on the business as his mistress. As you might suspect, the wife has an intense array of feelings. On the one hand, she feels proud to be married to such a successful man. She may feel that she's living a lie, that the world thinks that she and her husband have an ideal marriage because he carries great prestige, and is charming and pleasant in public, but they may have had separate bedrooms for twenty years. The public may not know that there is virtually no intimacy between them.

"Sometimes, in such a situation, when the father dies, the wife and mother may side with the younger children against the oldest son and heir apparent. The implication is very clear: the mother is still angry about what her husband did and did not provide. But her way of retaliating is indirect. She can't reach her husband any more because he's dead, so she sets up her son as the target. The heir apparent of the business is going to be the heir apparent psychologically, too, according to the wife, and she will team up with the younger children and make use of stock issues, equity interest, and control. When the anger of being spurned for a mistress is never dealt with and never managed, it leaves a scar which may never heal."

With a husband away all the time, the role of child rearer is a foregone conclusion. This may take two decades of a woman's life, and the woman has the total responsibility not only for child care, but for disciplining the kids as well.

One respondent, heir to a supermarket empire, described the parameters of his mother's world, as he saw it:

"She had her turf. He had the business and she had us, and she had to convince herself she got the better part of the deal. At the time, she really wanted to go into the business, but she had to settle for us. In every case in which I've talked to someone about this, I've found that founders are unlikely to share their innermost thoughts with anybody, but if they tell anyone, it's their wives.

"Consequently, wives do have a quasi-power behind the throne, but it's not true power. They have at least a moderating influence in some instances. They generally do present the human side of things, as women often do who are married to entrepreneurs, who can be very tough characters. I think the wives have the toughest job because they have to deal with all of us, and there's nobody really to help them. Often they haven't had their fair share of time either before they start producing heirs."

There are, of course, exceptions. Not every founder's wife was passive. Some had opinions, and voiced them, and their opinions carried weight.

Marla Schaefer, for example, of Claire's Stores, Inc., the accessory chain founded by her father, talked about her mother, who refused to mediate between the generations.

Said Marla: "My mother always told me, 'This is your father and you've got to get along with him, so do it.'

" 'But, Mom,' " Marla would say. " 'You talk to him so well. Do it for me.' But she never did, and I'm glad. I had to get there myself."

And yet Marla's mother spoke up when she considered it to be important. Marla told me: "My mother is a very level-headed woman and I think he respects her opinion. Because she's not involved in the day-to-day running of the company—although she sits on the board of directors—she gets the whole story in bits and pieces from other people and then she assesses it. I think she's able to give her assessment of a situation from an outsider's point of view, which can be very helpful. Sometimes she's able to speak to my father in terms that he understands when I just won't be able to talk to him."

It seems to me that Marla's mother makes very intelligent use of her special relationship with her husband: she acts as a reliable sounding board, and in addition has her husband's best interest at heart, which makes for a trusting relationship.

MOM-AND-POP PARTNERSHIPS

Traditionally, in start-up companies of a generation ago, the husband would be in charge of making the product; he, or perhaps his brother, would go out and sell it; and the wife would keep the books. She might continue in this occupation until the business expanded enough to hire a professional, or the kids started to be born, or both. The wife would then have a lifetime of child raising and housekeeping to look forward to, while her husband tended the business.

Although this model is, in fact, quite common among the families in my sample, it is not true universally. There are plenty of couples who go into business together, and stay in business together. These companies may be fruit-and-vegetable stands or much larger ventures—restaurants, publishing houses, graphic design firms, or crafts businesses are often founded by husbands and wives working in tandem.

It's not hard to imagine the sorts of problems that could arise with such an arrangement—for one thing, that's a lot of togetherness for two people to handle. A little too much of a good thing?

Benjamin Benson, in his book *Your Family Business*, talks about influential author Sharon Nelton and her book *In Love and Business*. Nelton interviewed many couples in business together for this study, and in it lists what she calls the potential "stress producers," common when married couples work together:

1. They have different work habits.
2. They have different management styles.
3. They have different business goals.
4. They have different approaches to money matters.
5. They don't successfully keep personal problems out of the office.
6. One or the other is easily offended and can't stand criticism from the spouse.
7. They work so hard that they don't have enough time together.
8. They're always tired.
9. The wife complains that not only does she have a full-time job, but is expected to manage the bulk of housekeeping tasks as well as child rearing.

But there is always a flip side, and a great many couples enjoy working together: they *like* the time spent with each other, and feel that being an intimate part of the work life of the spouse is a plus.

Sharon Nelton, in writing her book, had a goal similar to my own: she wanted to identify traits common to the most successful husband-and-wife business teams. Her results:

- Their marriage and the children's welfare have top priority.
- Each spouse is respectful of the other and tries to look at a problem from the other fellow's point of view.
- They communicate effectively.
- Usually, the spouses show complementary skills—each has his or her own province.
- The couple is mutually supportive and aim their competitive arrows at the outside world, not each other.
- And—most important, I think—the successful couple often have fun. They haven't forgotten to have a good time.

I agree with all these observations: they confirm similar traits one sees demonstrated by the extended family in a successful family business.

MOM IN CHARGE

If a husband dies unexpectedly wives of founder/entrepreneurs are forced to deal with more than homemaking and child-raising.

The mother of Italian shoe manufacturer Massimo Ferragamo had to pitch in when her husband died in 1963. At the time Massimo, the youngest child, was only three years old. As her six children grew to adulthood, each entered the business, bringing with them specialized experience and skills. In the process, the

164

company became an international presence, and expanded to fulfill the founder's dream of manufacturing not only shoes but all kinds of women's fashions and accessories as well.

Massimo Ferragamo credits the phenomenal growth of the company to his mother's strengths in the areas of both family and business: "After my father passed away, she sat at his desk and took care of a lot of things she knew very little about, just by using good sense and getting the right kind of help, which is very important. She had an innate business sense, which, if you don't have it, you can't gain it, even if you're a Harvard graduate. She guides herself by using this business sense, which I've always much admired."

Sometimes that mom who was the company's original bookkeeper-turned-homemaker is heard from again, and in a big way—upon the cataclysmic event of her husband's death. A spouse can inherit the business and not pay estate taxes (thus it becomes the problem of the next generation), so frequently—and we'll deal with this painful subject in the next chapter—in an attempt to stave off the IRS, the wife will inherit the business. Mom the one-time book-keeper becomes the Big Boss.

Yes, it has happened that a totally untrained widow decides to run the business with disastrous results, but there are plenty of success stories, too: Katharine Graham of the *Washington Post* springs to mind.

One can only hope that an intelligent management plan has been put in place against the day that the founder/entrepreneur is no longer around, and that the heirs, whether they work in the company or not, cooperate and compromise, keeping the good of the company firmly in mind.

"GOD, SHE'S FANTASTIC!" MOTHERS AS FOUNDERS

Until her recent marriage, Dominique Richard lived at home with her mother, real estate broker Alice Mason, on New York's Upper East Side. At the end of an interview filled with enthusiasm and laughter, Dominique hugs her mother, nearly lifting her off the ground, and says, "I think my mother's a star! And I'm her biggest fan. There's nobody in the business who did what she did. All those newcomers in the business—let's see them in thirty years and I'll be more impressed. And you know, she makes me think I do okay, and that's fine. She doesn't criticize."

In general, I found the daughters of the mother/founders whom I interviewed to be individualistic and confident—and they all seemed to have lots of affection for their mothers, which was reciprocated. Dominique Richard describes her enviable relationship with her mother: lying about, relaxing, discussing deals and gossiping, "being really good pals."

Alice Mason is equally enthusiastic about her daughter: "When I hear Dominique at meetings, I think, 'God, she's fantastic. I didn't know about that point she made. Is that the language you use today?' I don't even know the names of the people on the new listings. I don't want to know. But Dominique knows."

Georgette Klinger is another founder/mother of an only daughter who is heir apparent to her successful skin-care business. "My daughter is my eyes and ears," says Georgette of Kathryn Klinger Belton. "She is an extension of myself, and she does business in Los Angeles, where I do not care to be, in a culture that is alien to me. I am interested only in skin care, not in cosmetics. That is Kathryn's area."

This mother-and-daughter team lead a bicoastal life connected by phone, fax, and lots of transcontinental flights, but their closeness is obvious, and both agree that the separation may, in fact, enhance their relationship.

Bernadette Castro, who heads the sleeper sofa company founded by her late father, Bernard, was a mom long before she was a boss, and she has a clear grasp of what goes into both jobs.

Bernadette was raising four children when the tragic death of her brother forced her to combine the two careers in a way that educated her very quickly about what it meant to do both. Today, she can laugh about the difficulties involved: "I'm responsible for so many things now I'm stressed out altogether, and on top of it I really am a family nut and a neurotic mother. When I talk with women's groups, I tell them that my children have found two words to sum me up: not normal. This is not a normal house, we do not have normal dinners, and I am not a normal mother. In reply, I tell them, if you just do normal things, you can't expect to achieve great things. But, in times of great frustration, I ask myself, are any of these things I'm doing good enough?"

I think that the women founder/entrepreneurs whom I interviewed epitomized many of the good things that make family businesses work. They communicated well with their children, in most cases with their daughters; they were flexible enough to allow the next generation to learn and to make their own mistakes—the flip side of this was the real opportunity given to the kids to succeed; and they were at least willing to discuss their future plans for the company.

When the Kids Bring Mom Aboard

Not all family business moms were stay-at-homes—although that was the traditional role. One of my most unexpected finds was the pattern of mothers being brought into the business by their sons and daughters, frequently after the death of the CEO.

The three Karol brothers—of HMK Group Companies, a diversified business dealing with, among other products, steel, carpets, and office furniture—hired their mother, Joan, to work in the business after the death of their father. When the founder was alive, she played the traditional mother role, but during the period in which she was trying to come to grips with her widowhood, her sons convinced her to come to work for them.

"We call her Joan, not Mom," explained her son William. "She had played a somewhat submissive role with her husband and three sons, and was way down in the pecking order. When we were growing up, she would get stuck in the middle a lot, and was never very effective. But we loved her and we wanted her to be happy. With the help of a counselor, we got her involved in the business, and she became the person who planned our meetings. Now she's the director of public affairs."

Christie Hefner, chairman and CEO of Playboy Enterprises, also brought her mother into the business—a sign of modern times, as Christie's mom, and dad Hugh, are divorced. Sometimes fractured family systems are the norm and have to be adapted to the realities of the moment.

Said Christie: "I really grew up with my mother, and in very fundamental ways she helped give me the confidence to be a success in whatever I chose to do. She gave me a sense that I should try whatever I wanted to do, and that the likelihood would be that I would succeed in it. I came into the company at a young age, and became president at a young age, and one of the things people say when they meet me and hear me speak is 'You seem so comfortable and poised. Weren't you afraid?' I think the fact that I am those things has as much to do with my mother as anything else.

"She gave me absolute love and support in spite of her circumstances. Although she was divorced from my father, she raised me not to be bitter about him. She didn't create a rift between us in a way women often do who are left raising children and feeling abandoned."

Christie Hefner first put her mother into retail sales, and then into running programs in human resources. Through her highly developed facilitating skills, Christie has learned to manage her complicated family situation: "This year, my mother and her husband and my brother and me and my father, and now his wife and new baby and his mother, who's my live-in grandparent, can all spend time together. It's very pleasant and comfortable. In fact, facilitation is no longer required."

Meanwhile, in the Edelman family of Edelman Public Relations, in Chicago, daughter Renee reports on a kind of campaign in progress to bring her mother into the business.

"In all the years we were growing up, my father had an office for my mother and wanted her to work in the business, but she resisted. She said she couldn't see working for her husband, even though he had a history of promoting women and providing them with a good workplace. But I think she sees me in the business, sees that I'm productive and useful, and why shouldn't she be also? She's always giving ideas and working for free! The company just got the Weight Watchers frozen food account, clinics and all, and my mother keeps telling my brother she wants to work on it. He bought her a briefcase for her birthday."

In the infinite variety of behavior change that seems to occur naturally when two generations work together are all sorts of interesting role reversals, in this case the younger generation acting the role of mentor for the older. This is a very positive trend: it's what family businesses do best, when the younger generation wants to help expand the horizons of the older and the older is willing to risk learning something new.

Chapter

9

"In the Unlikely Event of My Death" —Unto the Next Generation

This chapter is concerned primarily with one kind of problem, the kind that takes place in the future but which must be dealt with today. The questions surrounding this problem-to-be are asked by the entrepreneur/founder: I'm getting older—where is my company headed? Who will take over for me when I retire so that the company will survive into the next generation? Do I have a management team in place now who can help my successor cope with any contingency? And, finally, have I prepared adequately for my own personal future? Is my estate plan as good as it can be, my retirement assured, my will in order, have I purchased proper insurance? Have I set up trusts? Would I do well to consider

171

establishing a foundation for fulfilling my dreams beyond the business?

Each historical era has problems specific to it—for my generation, they include the imminent retirement of our parents, the entrepreneurs who came to prominence after World War II, when money was cheap and the markets eager for new products. The youngest of this generation are now in their sixties, most of them in their seventies and older. Do I think that all of them have cheerfully asked themselves the questions listed above, and made sure that sensible answers were forthcoming? Of course not.

Not that they haven't been advised to do so by just about everyone. My younger respondents have told me again and again that discussing questions of succession with their parents is one of the hardest tasks befalling the upcoming management generation. Often their parents just don't want to think about it, giving new meaning to Scarlett O'Hara's immortal decision to think about it tomorrow.

A few years ago, members of the Young Presidents' Organization were surveyed about their feelings concerning retirement: these were relatively young people—at the time they averaged mid-forties—so they had to look down the road quite a piece. About 40 percent of them ran businesses wholly owned and controlled by the founding family.

When the answers were tallied, founders by and large said that they never wanted to retire; and their relatives who worked with their companies agreed. None of them felt that they should have to leave because of age: ill health or boredom seemed to be about the only reasons they would step down.

Nonfamily presidents had totally different reactions—more than half were actively looking forward to retirement.

Obviously, the attachment of the founder/entrepreneur to his or her company was deeply felt. And having built a corporation in their own images, many identify so strongly with their creations that they cannot step aside, not even for a child.

Who wants to purposefully remove himself or herself from the center of the action? It means slowing down . . . maybe an unwanted retirement . . . and finally thoughts of one's own demise. These are not family conversations that anyone wants to have. In some cases, the founder resists such talk until it's too late. We all know the horror stories:

- The founder dies with no estate plan in place. The heirs expend all their energy and ready cash in legal battles, no one minds the store and the business either must be sold or goes down the drain.
- The founder's son spends most of his adult life running his family's small-boat sales business. The company supports his family and his parents. He has no formal agreement with his father; it is understood that he "has been taken care of."

 The father dies, and what does the son discover? The business has been left to his mother, who has never been involved in the company in any capacity. He now effectively works for her, and he has a feeling that she is going to have her own thoughts about how things should be run.

- At the age of sixty-five, the founder decides that it's time to give over the manangement of his beloved company to his children. His son becomes president, in charge of day-to-day operations; his daughter, a vice-president—strategic planning is her bailiwick. But Dad is still CEO, and retains control of his stock. He has really given his children nothing—they have responsibility, but no power. With no power, they have no real authority within the company. The founder still calls the shots no matter what lip service he's paid to the new arrangement.

- Or, the flip side of the coin, the founder/entrepreneur has given actual control of the company over to his kids. He goes to Florida, to enjoy some fishing and sun and good times.

    Like a great many retirees, he just hates it. But any conversations with his offspring about coming back on board are rebuffed—as far as they're concerned, the transition has been made and there's no going back. The kids' suggestion that he take up a hobby is not a success. A hobby to him is a pastime suitable for small children. Any occupation should bring in money. Without that challenge to measure himself against, his daily activities seem trivial and frivolous. His ego is bruised and his self-esteem is slipping. Retirement is purgatory.

There are as many additional stories as there are companies that never make it to the next generation. And no amount of planning will guard against virulent sibling rivalry, or greed, or chicanery, or stupidity, any of which can lead to the destruction of a company during the transition period.

There are two separate issues to be considered when we talk about authority shifting to a new generation: *succession planning* and *estate planning*. Each of these has to be arranged by the founder/entrepreneur, or whoever is in charge of the managing generation. Succession has to do with *who* is going to take over the top spot—this can be done while the founder is still alive—and estate planning governs ownership and distribution of assets after the death of the founder.

Is all of this important? It is if you want the company to remain in the family. Let me remind you of the average survival rates of family businesses as reported in *Nation's Business*, the publication of the U.S. Chamber of Commerce: two-thirds of family businesses survive to the second generation. By the third generation only 13% of those businesses are still operating. Obviously, you cannot do too much planning if you want to make it to that third generation.

"THE FINAL TEST OF GREATNESS"

"The final test of greatness in a CEO is how well he chooses a successor and whether he can step aside and let his successor run the company." That's an observation by business management expert Peter Drucker—and one shared by many of my respondents, especially those of my generation.

In an ideal world, the founder should start to think about succession as soon as it is clear that the business is a going concern and there will be something material to pass on to the next generation. The founder's planning must include not only a choice of successor or successors, but must put in place all the legal and financial instruments that ensure smooth passing of the management baton. But in order to plan intelligently, if you are the founder, you must learn to control your fears:

- Fear of the leisure of retirement.
- Fear of being bored.
- Fear of death.
- Fear of possible financial loss if the business nose-dives after the founder's departure.
- Fear of living on a more-or-less fixed income.
- Fear of family conflict when the new team takes over. And that most deep-seated worry . . .
- Fear that your designated successors will be utterly incapable of filling your shoes successfully.

175

In fact your successors don't have to fill your shoes—they have shoes of their own by now, in fashions of their own choosing. Accepting the individual styles of your kids and other members of the new management generation is one of the most important things that you must do if you and your company are facing transition. New ways of doing things may not be your ways but they are not necessarily ineffective.

Also vital: I've said earlier that one of the structural advantages of a family business is its ability to enter into long-range planning. That's all very well to say, but now you've got to put this into practice.

Succession Checklist

You are the founder: is your struggle to figure out ways to pass your pride and joy on to the next generation worth it? Usually, it is. For the founder, the business can be a personal creation, almost a living thing. And the knowledge that this creation will be passed into the hands of your offspring does endow a kind of immortality—in any event, it's nice to know that one's interest is being picked up and developed further by the next generation. The intergenerational ties of family can be among the most emotionally satisfying that we experience as human beings.

If you really do think that tomorrow will never come, heed the words of business consultant Leon Danco, founder of the Cleveland-based Center for Family Business, who has spent an illustrious, lifelong career advising family businesses on difficult matters of succession. In commenting in *U.S. News and World Report* on the survey statistic that only 1 in 3 owners had drawn up a formal succession plan, Danco said, "I often have to remind fathers that though they are divine, they are not immortal. If you don't take care of the continuity of the business now," he warned, "then the executors will take care of it for you on the way to the funeral, four cars back from the flowers."

Danco and other well-known consultants who offer succession plans also like to offer checklists of dos (we know what the main don't is—don't do nothing) to be followed by the founder. Most of the items on these lists are commonsensical and give advice that's easy to understand but hard to follow. For example:

1.   Try to plan for succession as early in your career as you can. It's never *too* early, as any plan always can be changed later. Most entrepreneurs should start thinking about succession while they're in their mid-fifties and perhaps have children in their mid-twenties. Rule of thumb: It takes about five years to put a workable succession plan in place. It doesn't matter if the top job doesn't change hands for a very long time. After all, the next generation has to be trained properly. At least you're prepared for the unexpected.

2.   Designate a successor, and be sure that executive is being properly trained. This may be an interim person, perhaps not even a family member. There may be several top-management possibilities in your family—but the most likely of them might be only fourteen years old. Don't wait for that child to grow up. Unfortunately you must live as if tomorrow might be your last day on earth.

I did come across some creative alternatives to naming one child as heir apparent when it appeared that more than one had equal claim on the top job. The Modell brothers, Mitchell and Michael, of the sporting goods company, each has the title of president, although their areas of interest and responsibility are different.

And the family of David Finn, of the public relations firm of

Ruder Finn, which he founded with the now-retired William Ruder, share executive partnership in the company. The oldest daughter, Kathy, is president of the company, Amy is president of the New York headquarters, and son Peter is chairman of the executive committee and chief administrative officer. A fourth child, Dena, is not interested in management and is their editorial director.

The Finn children brought to the business advanced degrees, computer skills, and plenty of outside experience. Since they have become a part of management, working as equal partners, the company has doubled both sales and earnings.

3.   In training a successor, you must be certain that this person is given real *authority, not just responsibility.* A family member might earn respect by turning in a good performance, but only you can bestow true authority, and with it the power to manage effectively. If you're serious about delegating authority, you can't equivocate. Power once given should not be taken back.

4.   If you plan on keeping all the stock within the family, it's a good idea as you plan for the future to try to consolidate shares in the hands of those family members who actually will be running the company. This might involve buying back shares from outside shareholders—perhaps a nonfamily member who owns a few—or buying out family members who have financial equity but no other interest in the company.

5.   As your company matures and you move into your middle years, you ought to become a teacher yourself. It is really your job to see that those morals and values that you as a family have always espoused are understood to be standards to live by for the next management generation. Perhaps you should consider writing an ethical will.

6.   And have you checked your employee morale lately? One of

the problems with "plateaued" managers is that they lose touch with the needs and complaints of their employees. Have you really established a work force that is loyal and dependable? Check it out: it's going to be very important to your successor.

7.   Is the internal structure of your company all it should be? Is your organizational chart clear? Does everyone have a clearly defined place on that chart and is company hierarchy understood by all?

8.   Do you have an outside board of directors to keep you from straying from the hard truth? A group of advisers for the same reason? They will be needed by the next generation. Old pros who know your company will be gold.

9.   In planning the future, accept a worst-case scenario. If you have two children who have never gotten along, the situation will not change miraculously when you are no longer involved in the business. Do not, for example, give them each 50 percent. You must choose one, and make sure that child has a controlling interest when it comes to actually running the company.

10.   Do not dismiss the thought of selling the business. It might make good sense financially. You may have no family members talented enough to manage the company competently, and it would be foolish to throw away a lifetime of hard work and equity when a profitable sale could be possible.

11.   Talk to your family. Your decisions, after all, affect their lives directly. They should know your plans in detail. They also should be given a timetable: you must decide when you will relinquish control and what you think your future role in the business ought to be. And once you've decided, and discussed your plans in depth, you should really try to stick to the agreed-upon schedule. If you do not, you're going to face an awful lot of resentment within your palace guard.

Trouble Spots

We've already discussed the most serious obstacle to sensible succession planning: it lies with the founder and his or her reluctance to face reality, and mortality, and perhaps even the grown-up competence of the children.

But reluctance can be overcome—and eventually, with the urging of impatient children, and the advice of anxious tax accountants who want estate planning in place, the founder may see the necessity of thinking seriously about what will happen "if the time comes."

Reluctance of the top person to plan is not the only obstacle to smooth transition, however. Some unhappy possibilities:

- The founder does have a succession plan in place. But that's something to think about in the future—the founder is only sixty years old and in good health. Yet sales have been flat lately and company executives are beginning to fear that perhaps the boss just doesn't have it anymore.

  Stewart C. Malone and Per V. Jenster, writing in a recent issue of *Family Business Review*, call this the "problem of the plateaued owner-manager." This may occur in a business that furnishes the same product year after year, to the same customers, using the same delivery methods. Entrepreneurial excitement is dead, although this may not be recognized by the founder. The authors point out that "the real danger lies in providing exactly the same product or service to the same customers, since few industries are so stable that requirements do not evolve over a decade. The identical product and customer mix may indicate that the firm is not recognizing the changes that are occurring in the marketplace," a situation that can cause business death if it's not recognized.

- The founder may be old, or sick, or—worse—mentally incompetent. This can lead to some very nasty legal business, which sometimes cannot be avoided but is always destructive to family relationships.
- Divorce is very frequent in our society today. A great many founders have second, or third, or more spouses. My parents divorced and my father has remarried. And what about the founder's children? I've been married and divorced and find myself with plenty of company within my generation.

    For every split, there's an ex-spouse, and sometimes ex-step-children, and ex-in-laws. Any of these may feel that they have rights—moral or legal—and everyone could end up in court, a most nonproductive pastime.

    Prenuptial agreements are not to everyone's taste—some new spouses resent them more than others. And yet the prospect of family stock being tossed about in a divorce settlement is very unappealing. Some companies have gone so far as to require that family members, if they marry without a prenuptial agreement, tender their stock shares back to the company.

    Second spouses also may become a problem to the founder's children, especially if these spouses have children from a first marriage and inherit part of the company on the founder's death. I'm sure any family business member who has found himself or herself in the unenviable position of legal confrontation with the widow or widower of a deceased parent feels as if they could write a book about the experience. At bottom, such goings-on are never good for the health of the business, which after the death of the founder needs all the help it can get.
- The emotional health of the family business is not good.

    In my role as business advice columnist for the magazine

Family Business, I recently got a letter from a reader who told me that she would like to spend less time running the family textile business that she had inherited from her husband after his death. But she feared, as a great many entrepreneurs do, that "if I leave there will be a lot of competition between the two couples for control of business." Her son and daughter and their two spouses had joined her in the company, and although they all got on harmoniously at the moment, she feared for the future.

Because she was going to be around for the transition, and could control the process up to a point, I did not think that in this case she had too much to worry about. But her anxiety was not irrational. The prospect of power and money does not always bring out the best in people, and no one can predict accurately what will happen in the next generation once it's their turn to lead. That's when all the cracks in the facade of family togetherness may deepen and pull apart. And it's also when personality flaws—secrecy on the part of the founder, for example—or destructive family dynamics (uncontrollable sibling rivalry comes to mind) can doom a succession plan before it's even formulated.

YOUR NEW MANAGEMENT TEAM

Sometimes the best-laid succession plans go awry. We have to look no further than the history of Curtis L. Carlson, whom I interviewed last year and whose travails are in the media a lot as we go to press.

Curt Carlson, seventy-seven years old, is the founder and sole owner of the gigantic Carlson Companies, a hotel, travel, and marketing giant. He has been used frequently as an example in studies of succession as a man who decided his son-in-law, Skip Gage, was the best-qualified executive he knew to be his heir apparent.

Carlson was full of enthusiasm for a while, but in the spring of 1992 it became clear that things were not going smoothly in the Carlson executive suite. Son-in-law Gage was out—although amicably, it appears—and Curt Carlson's older daughter, Marilyn Nelson, appointed the new heir apparent.

Carlson has two daughters, and they seem to be in line to inherit the company when he dies. Will Marilyn still be first in line when that happens? And if she is, what will that mean to family relationships—to her ousted brother-in-law and to her sister, Barbara Gage? And will Carlson Companies continue to succeed? Only time will tell.

If Curt Carlson is still trying to figure out his best possible succession plan, it seems clear that you can only follow your best judgment in putting a new team in place. Sometimes unexpected events change the picture totally, and you all have to go back to the drawing board, but that's no reason not to do the best you can now. Some advice:

- *Be clear about your intentions.* You must name a successor and ensure that person really will have the power to make decisions. He or she must have voting shares. For example, never leave a company fifty-fifty to your two children. Trouble will erupt eventually no matter how well they get along.
- *Keep your nonfamily executives and board members solidly in the picture.* The nonfamily employees should be reassured that their jobs will survive the transition, and the board members apprised of any changes that might affect their duties.
- *Make your intentions known.* If you're going to retire, say

when; if not, make that clear, too. Then, stick to your departure date. And stay away. You may be sought out as a consultant, which is great, but let the request come from the new management team. You still have a financial interest in the company, but, day-to-day, it's their worry now.

Management professor Wendy Handler has pointed out that when the succession procedure, and potential retirement, are viewed as a challenging learning opportunity, resistance is often minimal.

YOUR RETIREMENT

A word about your future: You don't have to overreact to time's passage. I'm only urging that you have a sensible succession plan in place; I'm not suggesting that you have to move on at the age of sixty, or seventy, or eighty.

If you think retirement will bore you to tears, don't retire. Or, leave one company and form another. Spin off a division from the larger company that you're giving to your kids.

A great many active entrepreneurs really don't want to play golf. If your health is good, your only limitations are those of imagination. You can have a whole new life after retirement.

Several of my interviewees—of the founding generation—were contemplating creative pursuits, sometimes after years of informal study. Robert Matt of Ethan Allen is studying philosophy. Real estate developer Samuel LeFrak is involved with underwater archaeology and paleontology. Mansfield Industries' Koke Cummins hasn't had enough business, and wants to turn around another ailing company. Henry Bloch is becoming more active in the civic affairs of Kansas City; and my father also is active in civic activities, as well as with several venture capital start-up companies. Then there's his dream-come-true, the Sy Syms School of Business at Yeshiva University.

MONEY MATTERS

Your business's financial health, now and in the future, is tied in with your own now that you're thinking about succession and possibly retirement. You must be assured that your own finances are secure as well as those of the company. And you want to know that both your family and the business will be in good economic shape when you're no longer around. One of the reasons that so few family businesses make the transition from generation to generation is that without careful planning, estate taxes can force the liquidation or sale of a thriving but cash-poor company.

It is not my purpose in this book to discuss your financial options in technical detail: that's what tax consultants and estate planners are for, and specific information becomes dated very quickly. The tax code changes constantly, and so do the guidelines for inheritance. Be advised that you should have in your corner up-to-date accountants and lawyers who will review your financial situation frequently.

Some choices you should consider as you review your various options:

1. *You could sell the business.*

It has struck me that a great many second- and third-generation members of successful family businesses end up spending their time learning about resource management rather than about the business that made those resources possible. That's perfectly all right—it's fascinating to manage money—and it may be that the best choice for all concerned would be to find an eager buyer for your company and cash out.

It may be that the decision to sell is a painful one. Even if you want to keep your business going as long as possible, the company may be too small to compete in your particular market, or perhaps there is no family member who is qualified, or willing, to take over.

Whatever the reasons applicable to your family business, once the decision to sell has been made, you have to look for the correct buyer. Where should you look for that buyer? And who should it be?

- *The company could be sold to outsiders.* If this is your choice, you might look to your competition. They probably know all about you, and your strength might bolster up their weakness.

  You don't want to sell your company only to find that your profits disappear into the pockets of the IRS. This traditionally happens if you sell your assets—not your stock—which then are valued at the sales price. Your capital gains tax in this situation could be extreme. It is more advantageous for you to sell stock, because assets are priced at their current value, which you have already depreciated for tax purposes.
- *The company could be sold to your children.* You could sell it to them outright, or in installments, or through a private annuity. With the latter, your children's financial obligation extends only until your death. Be sure you get good advice about the tax implications of these various schemes.
- *The company could be sold to your employees.* Some families are trying a relatively new method of disengagement and selling their businesses to their employees—these are ESOPs, or employee stock ownership plans.

  This is an employee benefit plan, a kind of deferred compensation scheme, that invests primarily in stock of the employer corporation.

As ESOP is a "defined contribution plan": the employer's contribution is defined and the employee's benefit is variable. Each participant is credited with an appropriate number of shares of employer stock over the period of his or her employment. Upon leaving the company for whatever reason, the employee's account is distributed either to him or her, or the beneficiary, in shares of stock or in cash. The employee's benefit is dependent on the value of the stock.

An advantage to you is that the ESOP can borrow money to buy your stock, and you can defer tax on your capital gains if you sell at least 30 percent of the company's stock to the ESOP and invest it in an approved way—stocks, corporate bonds, another business.

2. *You could, if you're attracted enough to Wall Street, go public.*

We sold 20 percent of Syms, retaining a controlling share but gaining a lot of flexibility by having on hand liquid funds. There are other advantages: your management still remains independent; your employees can own a piece of the company, which is frequently excellent for morale; and there is always the potential for raising future capital if needed.

As with any stock offering, there is some risk, but at Syms we think that's acceptable—after all, in our case, 80 percent of the company is still in the hands of the Syms family.

In addition to the future of your company, you have other financial matters to contemplate. You must think of your personal financial security, which involves planning your estate. You want as many of your assets as possible to be transferred to your spouse or to the next generation. Your will, life insurance, plans for trusts and bequests all must be considered. You need the very best estate planning professional you can find. Remember that estate taxes can be as high as 55 percent—you don't want that, so think things through with the help of the experts.

Remember to discuss all the possible ramifications of the following with your professionals:

1.   *Estate tax.* These usually have to be paid within a year of your death, and obviously you want to plan to have enough cash on hand so that they can be paid. Some choices:

- If you've set up an irrevocable life insurance trust, these funds can be used to buy the owner's stock from his estate. The beneficiaries do not pay tax on these proceeds.
- It may be that you qualify for tax payments over a period of time—perhaps as long as fourteen years. Interest rates fluctuate, so you will need current advice on this plan.

Other ways to minimize taxes and plan for an orderly succession:

- Annual gift tax exclusion. You can start doing this years before retirement. You and your spouse can give each child $10,000 tax-free. Children who are actually working in the business can get company stock; those who are not can receive other assets of comparable value. This is especially helpful because the value of these gifts is then transferred out of your estate.
- Set up a buy/sell agreement. You ought to have a written agreement concerning who will have the right to buy whose stock in case of your retirement or death or other of life's vagaries, like divorce or serious illness.
- A larger transfer of assets. Each person is allowed to transfer up to $600,000 in assets either during his or her lifetime or at

death without paying tax—this is in addition to the annual $10,000. If your succession plan seems to be working well, and you approve of how the next generation is taking hold, you might consider this.

2. *Estate Plan Checklist*

Your goal is financial security for you in retirement, as well as a plan that will pay enough cash to your heirs to take care of estate taxes without draining the company treasury.

Don't overlook:

- Up-to-date wills for yourself and your spouse.
- Constant review of the current regulations governing state and federal estate taxes.
- A current plan to furnish cash to your heirs. Some possibilities include a life insurance trust or payment to the IRS over time.
- Gifts of stock to your heirs during your lifetime. Give careful thought as to whom you give stock. You're dealing with questions of future ownership of your company.

  Stock involves two principles: equity in the company and voting rights. When there are multiple heirs involved be sure that 51 percent of the stock is placed in the hands of the person or group whom you want to actually take control. *Never* give 50 percent each to two beneficiaries. Someone must have a controlling interest.
- Possibility of various kinds of trusts to minimize the tax burden.
- Most importantly, selection of a reliable team of financial advisers to help your heirs when the time comes. Ideally, these experts should know your business well, and a plus would be a working relationship with your heirs already in place.

  Included in this team are those designated as your executors, or, if a trust has been set up—in which property is given into the care of a third party for the benefit of your heirs—a fiduciary to deal with all the financial aspects.

There are various kinds of trusts that might be of help to you and your family:

- *A qualified terminable interest (QTIP) trust.* This might be set up if you want to make sure that your wishes as to the ultimate distribution of your assets are followed. In this kind of trust arrangement, the surviving spouse has no control over the final distribution of the property, but the income is available for his or her lifetime.

- *A charitable remainder trust.* You enjoy the income from your property during your lifetime—upon your death, the charity inherits.

- *A grantor retained income trust (GRIT).* This is a trust that is useful during your lifetime. By setting up this trust, certain property is transferred to your heirs, and you retain the income for your lifetime. The value of the property is excluded from your estate for tax purposes. At the end of ten years, if you are still alive, your beneficiaries inherit.

There is no way that you can plan for every possibility. But if you keep your primary goal firmly in mind—the financial health of both your family and your business as you all experience life's transitions—then the chances are good that your business will pass successfully to the next generation with its assets intact.

Chapter

10

The Nonfamily Employee

In this chapter I'll look at the nonfamily employee in the family business. We'll examine first the needs of the job seeker and then the employer, the family business.

THE POTENTIAL EMPLOYEE

Unless a company is very small (or a family very large), there are far more nonfamily than family members working in the business. So the chances are good that you work for one, have been offered the chance to, or will be.

If you now work for a family business, how comfortable are you with your future career potential? If you have an offer to join one, how do you decide if that specific family company is the place where you can fulfill your aspirations and make a real contribution?

Start off by understanding that the words "family business" offer only a partial description of a company. Is it small, medium, or large? Does it do business in an industry that is growing, stable, or dying? Are the employees and the executives uncaring, or bored to death, about their jobs and their company?

To describe a specific company, you must answer these questions. Add others that may be important to you. The result will be an accurate description that positions the company for your consideration. The term "family business" has now grown to mean something like "a small family business in a growing industry with enthusiastic, ambitious leadership." Or it might be "a large family business in a stable industry with dedicated but nonaggressive leadership." You now have a tool you can use to judge how you would fit in and the possibilities for the future.

You should add to the business criteria some lifestyle needs as well. Every company reflects a culture. What is important to you? Must a company be public-spirited, located in attractive surroundings, have a strict dress code, promote and encourage productive work practices?

Put together the answers to the business and lifestyle questions. Do they sound right for you? If they are, the fact that it's a family business should be inconsequential.

The final consideration should be timing. Are you at the entry-level stage, in mid-career, or at the policy level? In any case, you may find these general guidelines helpful in organizing your assessment.

An Entry-Level Job? What to Look For
I'm sure you've thought about more than the few guidelines I've listed here. But these are basic to almost everyone. Add to these —but don't forget them.

1.   Most companies are aware of the advantages of promoting from within. So look for a growing company or one that is large enough for opportunities to exist. Will your boss teach you what he has learned or will he shut you out? Will you be his enemy or his protégé? Is he capable of promotion or will you have to leapfrog him? You can probably get an accurate reading of his methods and attitudes by finding out what happened to your two predecessors. What they encountered, you will, too.

2.   What natural contact will you have with your boss's bosses? Will you have sufficient visibility to showcase your good work? Will you be able, at least by observation, to learn from them? Your entry-level job mission is to learn. Find a place that will teach you and then promote you. Find a working atmosphere that you enjoy and relate to.

I remember hearing the highest educational authority in New York State tell a graduating class at Skidmore College: "Don't be overly concerned about the specifics of your first job. After three years, 70 percent of you will be working for a different company —and after seven years, you will be working at a job or for a company that doesn't even exist today. You went to school to learn. Now go to work to learn. Pick your employer for what they can teach you."

Of course, the point is that it doesn't matter too much at this stage in your career if the business is family owned and run. You're not signing a lifetime contract, you're enrolling in a new school. Work hard and effectively—learn carefully and get ready for the next move up.

Middle Management: Time to Make a Difficult Choice

You're either a middle manager, or ready to become one in a public company. You get an offer from another firm to fill a job for which you're well suited. It's family owned and operated. What should you consider in deciding to switch companies?

We can assume that your present employer really has no more they can teach you, and that they don't have a similar promotion available soon.

First, you should consider all the criteria we described at the beginning of this chapter. Make sure your proposed new employer meets your requirements, which may have changed. If they do, it's time to think about what being in a family business can mean to you.

Let's get the most obvious disadvantage on the table right away. In a family business, you're almost certain never to end up as CEO. Or if you do, you will answer to the family who will retain voting control. The absolute control will always be in the hands of someone whose name matches that on the door. That sounds grim until we realize that more than 99 percent of the working population will never become CEO or wield unquestioned power wherever they work. Yes, you probably won't ever really run the show, but why worry too much about something that's unlikely to happen in a family or public business, anyhow. That's the disadvantage. There are many more advantages:

1.   Most important, you'll be working for a company that cares more about staying in business than making next quarter's figures. That's the family's job—to keep the business healthy for the generations to come. There's a great feeling of security for you, knowing your job won't disappear to solve a short-range

problem. If you're valuable to a family business interested in the long term, they'll find a way to keep you on board.

2.   You won't have to intrigue your way through the political infighting that is inherent to any organization. In a family business, there's less likely to be politicking—and if there is, it will be confined to family members. As a nonfamily member, you needn't be involved. Family member alliances will be among themselves. You can do your job and stay above it. And no matter how the internal struggles are resolved, you can't lose. Of course, all bets are off if you take sides. But why should you? You really have little to gain if your side wins, and it's bye-bye if they lose. These are family matters. Leave them to the family. And sleep better at night because you're not involved.

3.   Your personal growth track should be the same as at a nonfamily business. If the business is growing, your opportunities to advance are certainly there. Family businesses need good people as much or perhaps even more than public companies. Family businesses are far more likely to be meritocracies. Are you likely to be "blocked" because a family member is currently in the job to which you want promotion? If you're better at the job, you'll get it one way or another simply because structures are more easily adjusted in a family business. Job titles, descriptions, and responsibilities can be changed so that the right person is doing the right job. That can happen in a public company, too, of course, but somebody usually has to be sacrificed. In a family business, the family member won't be sacrificed, nor will you if you can do the job the family needs. It sounds paradoxical, but family businesses seem to be much more fair than most companies.

4.   In the beginning of this chapter, we talked about your crite-

ria for choosing a company. Now that you're at a higher level, make sure that the same criteria are still important to you. If it's a family business, those criteria are probably still important to the company. Even though the faces change over the years, the company culture really doesn't. The family, after all, was brought up together. Their ways of doing things are bound to be different, but their basic values stay pretty much the same over generations. So the intangibles, the lifestyle criteria, that are part of your good feelings about where you work can be expected to continue. And those good feelings add up to enjoying where you work and what you do. That means easier promotion, better personal relationships with your colleagues, and a great, satisfied feeling.

Syms and the Middle Manager

Before we move on to policy-level people in a family business, let's look at Syms and the middle manager. With large stores in fourteen states, we need hundreds of middle managers in our stores and corporate office. There are, after all, only five members of the Syms family employed in our business. Clearly, our own self-interest requires that we search out and hire the very best managers we can. If we don't, we can stop wondering about the survival of Syms into the next generation. There will be no business to wonder about. So I know why we want terrific employees, intelligent, dedicated, creative. Because good nonfamily employees are the underpinning of our business. We need their input, their hard work, their loyalty. Our commitment is to train them expertly and promote them fairly, exactly as if they were members of the family. In that familial atmosphere, we want to energize them, to encourage them to look for new ways of doing things, and to help them be most productive and personally fulfilled. We try to make sure our people know why they are being asked to do their jobs a certain way so they will find ways of doing them better. From educator (at Syms our term for salesperson) to top executive, we need the best professionals.

You're at the Policy-Making Level

Your business career has taken you to the top level. Whatever your title, you participate in the company's highest levels of discussion and decision-making. You may very well be in line for the top job, with only three or four aspirants on a par with you. Then, one day, you get a call from the CEO of a family business. They need someone with your experience to fill a top-level job.

Several weeks later, you've met with the family business CEO, as well as other family members and nonfamily key employees. You like the way they think and express themselves. You like the business and its practices. You like the look of the company's future. You like the financial package and the benefits. But you do have one problem: you have to give up your dream of running a company. If you stay where you are, there is a real possibility you may become CEO. And the truth is you like running for that job —it's stimulating, focused, and adds an extra dimension to your everyday activities.

If the top job is your first priority, assess honestly your chances of getting it. At the same time, consider what will likely happen if someone else gets it. Will your situation change as the executive ranks are shuffled? In other words, if you lose, what will you lose? That should be as much of a consideration as what will happen if you win. The only thing I am certain of is that things will be different whether you get the top job or someone else does. Think it through and make sure you have considered your position after the succession takes place.

Now let's think about your changing companies and joining the family business. The owners of the family business have told you that chief executive officer is not an available option for you. That job goes to the family. Clearly, the family needs your skills, knowledge, and experience. Your ideas will be respected. You will be a valuable senior manager. Your advice will be solicited and heeded. The only thing you won't have is the final decision.

But you will have many compensations. I think the most important is a sense of commitment that a public company can rarely provide. The business of a family business is perpetuating itself. Public companies often have several agendas. Success this year may be simply so that the business can be sold next year. The only commitment is to shareholders. Especially in today's world, the key reason for profits is to establish a higher selling price for the company. Long-term investments are hard to sell to a board of directors.

The same attitude toward immediate profits has a direct effect on how the company conducts itself. A family business, for obvious reasons, feels generally stronger about being a good citizen in the communities in which it operates. There is a familial relationship between the company, its employees, and the community. Inevitably, everybody who works for the company feels better about the company and thereby about themselves. A family business has a personal relationship with its neighbors. Believe me, it's a nice feeling to know that part of your everyday effort is going back to the public. And that's far more likely to happen in a family business. At Syms, we believe in putting back into every community in which we operate.

Finally, there is the advantage of easy accessibility to the leaders of the business. Using Syms as an example, any employee, at headquarters or in the stores, can reach my father by simply picking up the phone. It's even likely that the person answering their call will be Sy, not some intermediary. Time after time, I have found this to be a trademark of the family business. The layers are not overwhelming. They don't have to be. Structure generally doesn't get in the way, because it isn't necessary.

EMPLOYEE RELATIONS

At the beginning of this chapter, I promised that we would examine the nonfamily employee from two points of view—the employee's and the company's. When most entrepreneurs start a business, the pace is so fast and change so speedy there is little time to think of ways to get the best out of people. Most employee issues are answered with an abrupt "You're getting paid for it, so do it!" Clearly, this management style—the bully/dictator—is inappropriate and often downright disastrous for the start-up company that needs talented nonfamily members in order to grow. Younger entrepreneurs bring greater sensitivity and skills to the concept and application of management. Usually, it is my generation that brings the company into the professional management stage of business, a stage that is absolutely necessary if the company is not to die a premature death.

Money is not the chief reward for entrepreneurs. The chief motivator is personal independence. The founder has a close personal relationship with the company that permeates all of life. This intense involvement causes a blindness when trying to understand employee motivation. At the stage where the company exceeds the size that can be managed by one person, there are new skills needed that most founders have to learn.

Employee relations and human resources development evolve in most companies as they enter a more mature and growing financial stage: health care, day care programs, fitness programs, school tuition reimbursement, stock options, performance incentive plans, a way to participate in quality standards, committee knowledge of the company's financial health and growth plans, and, of course, training programs. The new workforce and most of the Baby Boom generation are searching for fulfilling and meaningful work, not a day's work for a day's pay.

The magnetism, enthusiasm, and confidence of the folk hero entrepreneur alone keep many loyal employees who feel energized by the quest of fulfilling the entrepreneur's dream.

Today, we lament the passage of a work ethic that made this country great. I have seen that with proper motivation, that work ethic has not passed. What is special about a family business is that employees are more interested in finding their extended family in the workplace. A family business already has a family—you just have to include your employees and make them feel part of your "labor of love."

We need to affirm the self-worth of employees. Just as a healthy family supports its members, the business must support the employees and reward productivity, loyalty, and outstanding performance. Don't be afraid to get close to nonfamily employees.

How Does the Company Choose the Right Job Candidate?
When I joined Syms, we had just two hundred employees. It was possible to know everyone by their first name. Today, Syms employs two thousand people, spread out across fourteen states. Recruiting the right person for the job has become critically important to our growth. You have to learn the techniques, put them into practice, and stick to specific guidelines.

Create a list of "musts" and "preferreds." You do this by talking to the person to whom the new employee will first report and anyone else who will have significant contact with the position. *Must* the job applicant have an M.B.A., or would you *prefer* it and not eliminate a candidate with good experience, a college degree, but no M.B.A.? *Must* she be fluent in Spanish or *must* he have five years' experience in a management position reporting directly to the president? Be clear about your *musts* and *preferreds*. Put the musts in your help wanted ad, let a headhunter know, and tell everyone in your company exactly what you are looking for to fill the job. One out of four jobs is filled through personal contacts. Be clear about the job responsibilities, tasks, and goals. Write them down and circulate the list.

Now let's say you've selected the best six candidates on paper. They all fulfill your list of musts and have some of your preferreds. Here's where your disciplined interviewing skills come into the success equation. An interview is an information-gathering process. During a first interview, say very little but ask many questions. Have a list of twenty questions prepared. I use the same list for all job categories. This way, over time I can see how the answers relate to candidate success. Take good notes. Believe me, when getting together to discuss a candidate with your father and uncle, you will not remember what the key answer was that convinced you "this is the one" unless you take notes. Ask open-ended questions. Before we improved our interviewing skills at Syms, we'd ask a candidate, "Do you like storekeeping?" Well, imagine someone saying no if they're sitting across from me and they need a job. Today, we'd ask, "What do you most enjoy about storekeeping and what are the three things you'd rather not have to do in a store?" So work hard to get questions that accurately reflect your concerns.

At the end of the first interview, give candidates two assignments. One, while they're in your presence, have them answer two questions in writing. Again, these should be open-ended questions. Give candidates only ten minutes to complete their answers. Second, ask them, in the next few days, to talk to people about your operation and send you a list of their concerns about the company. Assure candidates that there will be a second interview after you have received their list of concerns. When you next meet, you can see in writing who your candidates are:

1. Do they clearly imagine how they could add to your success?
2. Are their concerns narrow and self-serving?
3. Can they think on their feet?
4. What issues keep recurring in the answers written in your office and again in the home assignment?

Before calling the candidates back to discuss their lists of concerns, start your reference checks. This will take time. Take the time. Don't use the list of names the candidate gave you. Try to find the direct-report and speak to him about the strengths and weaknesses of the candidate. Now you're ready for the second "information giving" interview. This could include interviews with several people in your company. Compensation should not be discussed until the third and final interview, during which you must share your vision of the company and your expectations of the candidate.

Remember, your family business deserves the best management it can find. Many displaced managers today from large companies yearn for the opportunity to work in a place where they can make a real contribution, and a growing family business is a great place to do that. You don't have to settle for satisfactory people; you can hire excellent ones. Remember, an excellent manager is not expensive. They pay for themselves with their contributions to growth and by the burdens they will share. The clearer you are about the job that needs filling and how it fits into the larger picture, the more accurately you can describe it and later measure your selection.

Once They're on Board . . .

A family business must be particularly sensitive when determining to whom the new position reports. A sure way of destroying the best selection process is to have the position be directly responsible to all four family members working in the business. If this happens, the candidate will lose face because there is no clear way to be successful. Being an excellent manager of today's managers might be the first step in ridding your family business of some bad habits.

Don't make these mistakes:

- *Don't be a dictator.* If one person controls all decisions, authority becomes empty in the hands of other managers.
- *Don't be too rigid.* If there are rules for every possible situation, everybody stops "thinking" and managers can't grow.
- *Don't be exploitative.* Employees are not indentured servants. They can leave whenever they want, and they will.
- *Don't start fires.* Keep your criticism of family members within the family and don't use a nonfamily manager as your confidant.
- *Don't be secretive.* The more people know about and understand your plans for the business, the better they'll earn their salary and the more they'll feel challenged to contribute.

No matter what side of the fence you're on—nonfamily employee or family manager—success depends on planning and compromise.

If you're the employer, you must hire the best nonfamily executives you can find, but once they've joined up, you must be fair. You will have made certain promises to these employees, and they must be kept to the letter if you want to succeed in building a loyal, efficient nonfamily executive corps.

If you're joining a family firm, be sure that you understand not only what your responsibilities will be, but also your potential and limitations. Once you've accepted the restrictions inherent in working for a family firm, you can look forward to a rewarding association as a workplace member of someone else's family.

Chapter

11

How to Write
a Success Story:
Some Guidelines

When I started working on this book a couple of years ago, I wanted to find out what successful family businesses have in common. For me, "successful" means a company that is not only prosperous now, but also one that can analyze its own strengths and shortcomings to protect its future. This sort of business plans with foresight and makes use of talented professional management when necessary, hiring and keeping only those family members who can pull their own weight. It is adaptable.

In addition, the top managements in these admirable companies make an effort to take care of business first, before struggling with sometimes conflicting family priorities. In other words, they pay good attention to the needs of the business, and find ways to work through family controversy, which takes place even in the most tranquil, loving families and which can derail sensible corporate planning. These companies have established an *order of priorities*.

Finally, with the help of my respondents, I pinpointed a third common thread running through the management practices of most of the successful businesses: the ability to process conflict, whether it arises in day-to-day business dealings, within the family, or in that hard to define spot where personal wishes can rub up annoyingly against the hard spot of business necessity. Conflicts are normal and dealt with efficiently.

I would be surprised if a family business lasted for very many generations without encompassing all three characteristics that I mention above, which can be summarized as follows:

1.   *The management of a strong family business is adaptable.* It is not blinded by its own sense of right but is always searching out internal problems and trying to establish more efficient ways of managing. Research and development, no matter what the business, are key elements of the company that looks to the future. Successful long-term businesses try to predict future trends and how they can be utilized for the good of the family business.

2.   *A strong family business understands which priorities are important if the business is to prosper.* These businesses are not dogs governed by the wagging tail of *family* priorities, which frequently have very different, perhaps antithetical, needs and goals. In order for this criterion to remain firmly in place over the years, especially as power shifts from one generation to another, the family members involved in the business must have in common the primary goal of family business viability.

Priorities also have to do with the family business culture—

the shared ideals and common goals—that makes each family business unique. A family business might have serious community involvement, or fund a charitable foundation, or pride itself on the sort of family unity that takes care of all family members in need.

Or the family members could share a vision of business growth over the next decade, of greater success and market share. One of the great things about a family business is that there often is the shared sense that you're all in this together. And, being family, you usually know what the other guy is talking about.

3. *The ability of a family business to process conflict efficiently.* This is most important.

Conflict is a fact of everyday life—it exists on the street, in the office, and around the dining room table, as well as in any other area where human beings gather. In a family business, by definition, we combine the stresses of the office with the complicated relationships that exist within every family—resulting in the potential for really serious conflict and upheaval.

Companies that work well are those that—once again, with the consensus of family members—have in place techniques that are effective in defusing problems before they develop, or finding some area of compromise once they become full-blown.

CRAMMING FOR THE FINAL EXAM

Throughout this book I've tried to isolate similarities that successful family businesses hold in common. Most of them fit under the broad characteristics that I've outlined above. Clearly, if you are a member of a family business, or thinking of joining one, it would be useful for you to contemplate these common traits to see if they exist in your business.

My purpose in writing this final chapter is to review for you some of those characteristics, no matter what generation you belong to; no matter if you're a family member or an outside executive. My suggestions are based not only on my own interpretation of family business reality, but mirror the consensus of my interviewees as well. This is one case, I think, in which the majority opinion is probably useful. We want to know what works and what doesn't.

I have organized my review section using the guidelines suggested above, and divided my summaries into the three categories that I have isolated, all of them present in the mechanisms of workable family businesses. I think that you can find your own situation somewhere within my three sections.

Review the dos and don'ts, answer the questions, and compare your family business reality with the suggestions listed. See how you measure up—and how your company does, too. How can you improve? How can you set clearer corporate goals? Do you have in place the mechanisms for necessary analysis and conflict resolution?

And what about your own career? Is it on track? Do you feel confident that you have chosen correctly or is it time for reevaluation? (This question applies to the beginner as well as the manager facing retirement.) Surely I don't have to point out that you have only one life to live. *Manage* your career. Don't let the comfort of a sure berth in a family business rob you of the excitement and adventure of making your own way.

Don't drift. Become contemplative. Try to know yourself and what you really want. You can start by reviewing the rest of this chapter.

IS YOUR COMPANY MANAGEMENT
EFFICIENT AND ADAPTABLE?

This is your opportunity to give your company a passing or failing grade in the areas of efficiency, foresight, and ability to remain open to new ideas, whether coming from a new generation or the marketplace.

As the Founder/Entrepreneur . . .
Do you have a clear vision of the future that you want for your company?

1.   Are you and your family sure that you want the business to survive into the next generation? Obviously, this is basic to any long-term management policy; not every family is interested in the longevity of their company, seeing it rather as a cash cow to be disposed of at the highest possible price.

2.   If, like most founder/entrepreneurs, you do see your company continuing after you're gone, is your organizational plan in place? If you're large enough to have several levels of management, then the executives occupying those levels should know exactly where they fall on the organizational chart. It doesn't matter if they're family or not, lines of command ought to be clearly drawn. Is real management power in the hands of the new leader?

3.   Has your "message" been communicated to others in your company, especially to those younger family members who will come after you? Are your ethics and how they apply to business practices crystal clear to your family? You've spent a lifetime building a business in a certain mold—you should do everything in your power while you're still running the company to transmit your values to the next generation. You can't tell them how to

operate after you've gone—so you must tell them now why you believe it's best for the business and the family to do things the way they've always been done.

With the understanding that you do expect your business to continue into the next generation, have you given any thought to the early introduction of that generation into your company?

Much of a young child's introduction to your business happens automatically. For example:

- You no doubt talk about your business when you come home. Try to be positive. As I've pointed out earlier in this book, what child is going to want to join a family business that he perceives as giving a parent ulcers?
- Make the business fun. Visiting the office or the plant can be an event.
- Give positive reinforcement. It's likely that if you have a business that lends itself to easy, rote tasks, your child will either help out at the company or take a paying job there while in high school or college. It's important that, while the kids are not exactly setting policy, the work experience be agreeable— and they should absolutely be paid, just as any temporary worker would be.

Are you clear in your own mind—and does the rest of your family concur—who among your family members are welcome to join the business? And what they should offer if they want to be considered?

Some dos and don'ts . . .

- Do not welcome everyone. You don't want the losers of your generation suddenly arriving on your doorstep, after half a lifetime of job-hopping. And the younger generation certainly can toss up incompetents, too.

- Do be consistent in applying criteria to potential employees, whether family or not. Someone who comes bearing the family name is probably going to at least get an interview. After that, they need more: relevant education and work experience, just like nonfamily. It's especially important that family members —who may spend the rest of their working lives in the company—get job experience elsewhere first.

- Do demand that a potential family member show some interest in your business, or in some aspect of it. It's perfectly possible for a family member to think that details of the manufacture of inexpensive glassware for the lower end of the housewares market are not very enthralling, yet be totally turned on by the challenges of getting the family product into as many stores as possible.

- Do make sure that the potential employee, if a member of your immediate or extended family, shares in those family values that you hold—in concert with the other relatives who work in the business. A lot of kids go through a rebellious phase, but it's pointless to introduce into your company someone who is going to fight you on every issue, just because they *know* that they're right. It's also possible that their ideas may change as they get a little older. But, for now, you have other things to worry about than pacifying a firebrand from your kids' generation.

- Do not unilaterally abrogate whatever your family's custom is concerning in-laws. It may be that your daughter has married an absolutely terrific guy, and you'd really like to have him join you. But it has been traditional in your family to let in-laws fend for themselves in another business. What would happen if your second daughter marries a guy who isn't so terrific? Chances are, he would just *love* to find a steady job with you. Don't sow the seeds for predictable dissension. Let it alone, and in this case stick to tradition.

Once you've decided who in the family is hired, do you have managerial and personal guidelines in place to keep them happy— as well as yourself?

As the younger generation of your family comes of work age, you are going to have to adjust to thinking of them as possible contributing members of your company. If your business is of a reasonable size, you will have hired young people before, but perhaps not your nieces, nephews, or your own children.

If you haven't thought of any guidelines to help you—and they're already in Human Resources filling out forms—here are some basics to think about:

1. These children are adults now. No nicknames, no personal remarks, no reminiscences. Treat them as you would any other young person in the workplace and they will be very grateful.
2. When you look at these new employees, especially if they're your children, try to forget a lot of what you know about them. Put yourself in the place of a boss who doesn't know that Charlie was hideously overweight when he was a little boy, with a tendency to steal treats from the candy store.
3. Be consistent. Your children and their cousins deserve a fair shake. Company rules concerning salary, promotion, vacation, benefits, job performance, apply to everyone equally. And that means giving your children the opportunity to fall flat all by themselves if they can't cut it.
4. Let someone else do the dirty work. If you are truly consistent, and things *really* aren't working out with one of your kids, you might be placed in the unenviable position of having to fire your own child. You can be firm but sympathetic while, wearing

your Parents' Hat, you offer to help them get another job some-where else.

5.   Don't hover. Don't live vicariously through your children. They have lives of their own, or ought to, and they're probably seeing too much of you as it is. Unless you're the kind of family that has always enjoyed living in each other's pockets—allow them their privacy. You wouldn't call a nonrelated new em-ployee at home at eight-thirty on Sunday morning, would you? If you would, then forget this guideline. If you wouldn't, don't call your child, either.

6.   Let your child succeed. He or she should have a real job, with a salary suitable to his or her background. Compensation should be based on performance, and not seen as a sign of parental approval.

7.   Give your children some room to grow. They should not report to you, but to someone who is willing to advise, and train, and critique: a real mentor. Their self-confidence will increase if they are given doable goals. Success builds on success.

8.   Learn with your child. Don't leave all the current technology to the younger generation. A new computer? Sign up for the same course that everyone else is taking. You want to be able to speak their language, and you really don't need more than a smattering of understanding of high-tech equipment for that.

9.   Prepare also to teach, not lecture. Even if your kids are not reporting to you, you will want to pass along your experience, and philosophy, and vision for the company to the next genera-tion.

10.   Learn to communicate. Talk. No one will know what it is you want if you don't tell them. Be positive. If your children do something terrific, tell them. It won't spoil them. And everything you say to them does not have to be critical.

11.   And the flip side of the coin: if you're wrong about something, admit it. No one is suddenly going to think that you're a fool and, especially if you are cast in that traditional, autocratic mold, it might make you seem more human and approachable. Rule by terror usually doesn't bring out the best in employees.

12.   All siblings are not created equal, and they ought not to be treated as such. You also must consider the strong possibility of sibling rivalry. It's all very well to say that siblings must get along for the good of the company, but sometimes feelings of competition run too deep.

Make use of that competition. If your company is big enough, let each child have his or her own bailiwick. Do not have one sibling report to another—the results are usually disastrous. Many of the families that I interviewed solved the problem of more-or-less evenly matched siblings by giving comparable titles and assigning them to different departments. Sometimes it's best if siblings see each other more often at family dinners than at the office.

13.   Along these same lines, all children should not receive the same compensation. Sometimes one child will be promoted to a higher stratum than another, and the salary should be appropriate. That does not necessarily mean that one child will receive a bigger chunk of the company when it comes to dividing stock; it simply means that each child is paid according to his or her worth to the company.

Besides your philosophical vision for the future, have you thought about practicalities? What will happen to your company once you're no longer in charge? What will happen to you? Unpleasant though it might be, you have to think about retirement, and succession, and wills, and taxes, and estate planning.

Unfortunately, no one but you can take care of starting this particular ball rolling. You have to decide that it's time to:

- *Call the professionals—your tax accountant, your lawyer, the bank, your financial planner.* These are the advisers that are actually going to do the work. You do have to tell them what you want: your financial goals.

  You have personal goals, and business goals, which may be intertwined. For example, even though you're retiring, you may have it in mind to start another business—you need cash, and it has to come from your biggest asset, the company that you're leaving to your children to run.

  Even if you're not starting another business, you will need income during retirement. It is never too early to formulate an intelligent retirement plan, as well as delving into estate planning, just in case something happens to you.

  You want to leave the business in the best possible financial shape, of course, as you retire, and I have discussed your options in greater detail in chapter 9. Your advisers will set up the best tax-saving plan possible, using the most current information. It never is too soon to start thinking about personal and business finances, so it is quite possible that all your planning will have to be revised again and again as circumstances change.

- *Choose a successor.* This may be a family member if someone suitable is available, or a transitional professional manager if there's no one of age. But make your wishes clear—don't waffle. Everyone—including nonfamily executives—should be absolutely clear about what their position will be after transition. This is the time to make sure that professional management is ready to take over if the family should falter.

It is often these nonfamily executives who manage to save the business from going under during times of severe change.

- *Consult with your outside board of directors.* Not every family business has an outside board of directors, but they can be an enormous plus during a transition.

  Outside board members are usually CEOs of other companies, who meet several times a year to be part of your team for advice and counsel. If given the authority, they're the ones who can keep family members toeing the line, as they can analyze family business problems using the fresh perspective of the informed outsider.

- *Set a date for retirement, or gradual winding down, or whatever you've decided to do, and then stick to it.*

Some final questions for the founder/entrepreneur . . .

Have I learned true management skills over the years? Am I effective in my personal interactions, and do I really connect with my employees, be they family members or not?

As the founder/entrepreneur, you may find that the answers to the following furnish a little insight into your personal relations.

1. Do I listen to my advisers and employees—really listen, so that I truly understand what they're saying to me?
2. Am I tied into old ideas of primogeniture? Or can I look at all my children, including my daughters, and see them as individuals with different interests and abilities?
3. Am I arrogant? Do I know best . . . always?
4. Do I trust anyone completely? Even my children?
5. Can I accept criticism from anyone? Is there, in fact, anyone who would dare to criticize anything I might have done? Would I ever admit that I'd made a mistake? Have I allowed any

outside advisers to assume a position of oversight with enough power to actually call me to task?

6.   Am I completely closed to new ideas? Do I look upon the younger generation as nothing more than wimpy kids who always have had it too easy? Have I become more isolated as I've gotten older?

One of the most positive elements of a family business is the trust that family members put in each other. Yet, it is not uncommon for founders to ignore that feeling, to become more isolated, distrustful, suspicious of motives, and uncommunicative as they age and have to face the inevitable transfer of power to the younger generation.

If these barriers are erected, it is up to the family and outside advisers to do everything within their power to communicate with the person who is withdrawing—for the individual's sake as well as the company's.

Family businesses function best in an atmosphere of goodwill, shared goals, and, most of all, trust. Cooperation is key. Only by working together in harmony can those shared goals be realized and the family business survive and prosper.

As the Child . . .

Much of what was discussed earlier in this chapter from the parent's point of view applies to you—after all, you are affected by the management decisions made by the founder/entrepreneur.

But there are some questions that can be asked only by you, the child—and your parent could only guess at the answers, which you can furnish by looking deep within to see how you *really* feel about the trials and pleasures of working for the family business.

For example, there are questions for you to ask no matter how long you've been associated with the family business, or even if you are just thinking about joining:

1.   Do I like the business? Or if I don't care much for *what* we do, can I find satisfaction in figuring out how to raise efficiency or how to sell our product?

2.   Does my family have a history of fair play? Will I be compared constantly to my siblings' performance or will I be viewed as an individual? Will my unique talents be recognized, and will I be given a chance to develop them?

3.   I'm a woman. Is this going to matter in the long run? Or do I come from a family with a history of gender-blindness that expects achievement from the women as well as the men.

4.   Have I prepared myself properly for my family's business? Do I have an adequate educational background and, most importantly, have I had some experience in the marketplace, out on my own, where my name means nothing to my employer?

5.   If I join the business, does it appear on the surface that I might have a future? What has been the track record of those of my generation who have gone before me? Did they last? Did they leave in rage and desperation? Did they stay, and do they seem contented? Do they have real jobs, with responsibility and accountability? There is every reason for me to think that my experience will be similar.

6.   How do I get along with the family members already in the business? Will I be working for a parent? What has our emotional history been up to now? (Be very wary if it's been nothing but strife and strain since you were twelve.)

Are my siblings already on board? Have we had a mutually supportive relationship growing up? Can I count on them, or is our usual interaction based on competition and conflict.

7.   Do I have the qualities that will benefit me if I decide to join my family in the business? Do I have the sense to listen—and to learn from the older generation—or do I, the product of a fancy education, have my own ideas about how things should be run? Do I have the stomach and stamina for really hard work? And for work that might not be creative or stimulating? In other words, will I be willing to put in my time at the bottom of the managerial heap?

8.   Can I work for someone? Can I feel real respect for someone more experienced than I? I never really have had to answer to a superior for my actions—can I take criticism without blowing up? Or crying? Will I see supervision as a learning experience? Am I ready to be in the family business and not be boss, reporting to a sibling who may be younger?

9.   Finally, do I have the patience needed for me to put in my time, to learn, and to build a reputation based on my own performance and not on my family's name.

It takes time to achieve respect from coworkers, and you have to achieve successes on the job before management will listen to new ideas. You have to pay your dues, and should keep a low profile until you do.

WHAT ARE YOUR FAMILY'S MOST IMPORTANT PRIORITIES?

Most family businesses have priorities that are well known to those who work in the business: these might encompass business goals, policies concerning charitable giving or interaction with the community, or future plans for family members both within and outside the business.

Priorities can involve anything at all having to do with the way you live and conduct your business, but they will remain important only so long as they are understood and shared by all the relevant members of your family. Priorities are an important part of the common culture that we've talked about earlier—it's the shared vision that smooths over the cracks caused by occasional and inevitable conflict.

Priorities may have been codified in some way—actually written down in a statement of purpose, or as the founder's vision of the future. Or, instead of formal exposition, you may discover that priorities are simply, and almost unconsciously, interwoven into the family's unspoken cultural tradition: "We've always done it that way."

Following are basic questions to ask if you are a family member trying to understand your family's priorities in order to figure out if they match your own, and if you're comfortable with the corporate culture of your family business.

1.   Does your family share a strong moral code—is doing the right thing part of their reason for living? And do you share these ethical concerns? Be honest with yourself. You may not. You may really think that there is not much room for overriding ethical standards in the workplace. If your ideal work environment is a little more dog-eat-dog, then find a job outside the family business. You will find your relatives annoyingly pure of heart.

2.   Do you, in fact, also have a strong internalized need to help others? If, for example, you were brought up with the idea that it's important to serve the community, then you may share your family's enthusiasm for helping those less fortunate than yourself. The family business may encourage your participation in all sorts of volunteer activities: there may be a family foundation whose work interests you, or perhaps family members are urged

to become involved with community volunteer education programs. Or maybe you will be given the option of starting your own program, with help from company personnel and perhaps some seed money. If you're involved with a family business, you often have the luxury of making a long-term commitment to the project of your choice.

Part of your family's priorities are involved with how you do business—the ethics understood by all, what is expected of all employees in their interactions both within the company and with outsiders, whether vendors or clients. As a family business member, you can answer these questions automatically: Is the customer always right in your company's view? Is a promise your bond? To what lengths will you go to satisfy contract provisions to the letter?

You know before you even think about joining the family firm whether your own sense of what's important in corporate culture is shared by your family. If it is not, then you probably should not consider joining the company.

But there are other sorts of priorities important to a family business—ones that have to do with the business itself and that might affect you if you work for the company.

1. Do you, for example, agree with the long-term plans for the company? Are grandiose expansion projects in the works that you think the market will not be able to support? Do you believe that the best management possible is in place—do they have your total support or do you perhaps think that you can do better?

2. And what about your *personal* priorities? Are they at odds with the company's? Perhaps you're looking forward to retirement and want to cash in some of your equity in the company. Can the business afford to buy you out?

I could give hundreds of examples of priorities that might be important within your company—it almost doesn't matter what the specifics are. What does matter is how your own priorities dovetail with those of the company. A good match, and you may have found a lifetime home in the family business; a fundamental mismatch, and you shouldn't even try to adapt. Find a more sympathetic environment for you, and give that company the enthusiasm and devotion that you could give only reluctantly to your own family's business.

HOW DOES YOUR
FAMILY PROCESS CONFLICT?

Conflict just *is*—every family is going to have to deal with disagreements of varying intensity at one time or another. The trick is to defuse the conflict before it turns into deadly warfare and saps everyone's energy, forcing you all to turn your attention away from the most important thing that you as a family ought to be doing: taking care of business.

There is help available for you—these techniques are tried and true, and most of my respondents have had hands-on experience with one or more methods for keeping the peace.

Remember: Nothing can ever be accomplished without talking face to face. Communicate. If this is not a natural way to interact within your group, force yourself to break the ice. Meet with that older brother who has been grunting at you for years. Tell him your gripes in person. The results may surprise you, and sometimes years of icy silence can be swept away with one honest conversation. In fact, if you can learn to talk with each other, you might not ever need outside intervention.

But we live in the real world. Miracles do happen, but it is much more likely that the brother who has been grunting at you for years will look at you with horror, mutter something unintelligible, and leave the room, slamming the door.

So much for face-to-face communication. You're not going to reach rapprochement through your own efforts. You need to bring in the heavy artillery. It's time to get the input of others.

Those "others" might be members of your own family.

There are several ways in which your family may be able to calm troubled waters. Many families make regular use of:

- *The family council.* This is usually a meeting of family members—sometimes including only those who are actually involved in the company, but more often welcoming every relative who has a financial stake in the business and their spouses. These councils may meet a few times a year, and this is the opportunity for grievances to be aired and solutions proposed. Here is where the vision and philosophy for the company's relationship to family members should be clearly spelled out. There are bound to be almost as many agendas as members: those not in the business want more income; parents want children promoted. Agendas must be agreed upon before the meeting, with everyone invited to submit topics.

  Sometimes social pressure can be brought to bear to solve an otherwise intractable problem. There may be no right or wrong, just a difference of opinion. In those situations, you simply have to agree to disagree and *must* compromise.

- *The family retreat.* Think of this as a philosophical vacation. Usually, families that use this method of communication find someplace isolated, home ground to no one. Change of venue often leads to some shifting of usual relationships—greater familiarity can foster new understanding.

If a family has a history of real hostility, which simply will not die, it is good sense to bring an outside observer—a facilitator—along to help the family keep to the subject at hand and to defuse any personal attacks that might arise.

The "others" to whom you turn for help in improving communication might be outsiders:

- *The board of directors.* The board may have family members on it, but it's always wise to include some who are not related. Other CEOs make the best choice.

  This group has the best interest of your company at heart. They have the perspective of knowledgeable outsiders and know all of you quite well. Members of this board are obvious choices to advise parties to a dispute that can't be settled in-house.

- *Family advisers.* This might be a more casual, ad hoc group than the board of directors, but, once again, these people probably are familiar with your problems and they can frequently be of help in forcing some sort of agreement. At bottom, the disputants must have a certain amount of good will for the company, if not for each other, and wish for a settlement of the problem.

- *Facilitator.* This is a trained counselor who is either a family therapist or a reputable family business consultant who keeps you to your agenda and knows how to defuse hot issues.

- *Professional help.* Depending on your problem, you will summon the correct professional: legal problems, your lawyer; money matters, your accountant; problems envisioning the future and how your business can thrive in it, a market research futurist.

In fact, it doesn't matter what avenue you take so long as the problem is resolved. It is very difficult for a family business to absorb and synthesize any kind of long-running strife because its basic structure presupposes cooperation and taking care of the other guy. A kind of working harmony simply must be achieved if the family business is to do what it does best: use the family as an instrument for mutual aid and creative input and economic growth. A family business can only succeed if its members understand their family's priorities and are willing to give up a little of their own interest for the greater good.

When it goes well, the family business experience gives you a feeling of completeness, fulfillment, and joy that I can only describe as "the best." So start today—refuse to let your career pass you by. Join your family in an enterprise and make history together.

In closing, I'd like to share some insightful comments made by my respondents—comments about their experiences in family businesses:

> "The business started to prosper as I put effort into it. We grew to a point where we were making very significant profits, and we really had put together a team to be proud of. I can hold my head high and I feel self-respect for what I've done over time."
>
> —O. M. "Koke" Cummins, President,
> Mansfield Industries

> "I wanted to show nonfamily members that I was here because I could contribute and that I was worthy of the position that I was holding at the time. I think that I did earn their respect."
>
> —Tom Bloch, CEO,
> H&R Block

"The joy of a family business is that you can control your life, as opposed to letting the business control you. I want to be in a business where I control my destiny."

—Richard Edelman, President,
Edelman Public Relations

"I really went into the business to help my father and to help the family—and it's been a really rewarding experience for me."

—Shelley Roth, President,
Pierre's French Ice Cream Company

"I would never sell the business until I had had an in-depth talk with each of my children, because if there was just a glimmer in one of them, I would want to present to them what their grandfather gave to me. To come into a business that's already established, that has already taken its knocks, that has credibility and name recognition —that's a great gift. But you have to love it and you have to want it—I would never throw it away."

—Bernadette Castro, President,
Castro Convertibles

"There are times when the whole family's together. We know that we'll always be together then. We don't take Christmas and Thanksgiving away from each other. And we all go home to South Carolina on Labor Day."

—Sylvia Woods,
Sylvia's Restaurant, New York City

"And I can get away with saying things that others could get fired for saying. I would never do anything behind her [sister Karen, who is company president] back to intentionally undermine anything she's trying to do. But if I think there's a better way of doing it, I'll tell her what I think. And then she'll consider it. And that's very positive."

—Jackie Caplan, Vice-president,
National Sales, Frieda's Finest Produce

"We don't have that much conflict. And we can have an open discussion because we all respect each other. We all really enjoy being with each other. We'd rather be with our family than with anybody else."

—Lynn Roberts, Vice-president of Advertising,
Echo Design

"As far as caring for people, I think the people in this company know how much they're cared for, as if they were in a family."

—Nancy Lampton, Chairman and CEO,
American Life and Accident Insurance Company

"I've always thought that an enormous amount was done for me. I consider Martha [her mother] a creative source, so I was very fortunate to have all that."

—Lynn Phillips Manulis, President,
Martha, Inc.

"Nothing's better in life than being your own boss, nothing. I don't care what you do."

—Dominique Richard, Real estate broker,
Alice Mason Ltd.

"If you treat your family members in an open-minded way, you're going to hear things that improve not only your company but yourself. A family that can do that, a company that can do that, in my opinion is a very powerful place to work—much, much more fun than a publicly owned entity run by gray minds and gray suits."

—Steve Karol, President,
HMK Group Companies

Index

About the Author

Marcy Syms is president and chief operating officer of Syms Corp., the chain of twenty-nine off-price apparel stores founded by her father, Sy Syms. After work experience in public relations and communications, she began her career with the company in 1978, developing the marketing program that introduced Syms into the Washington, D.C., area; today there are Syms stores in eighteen markets.

Marcy Syms lives in New York City and works in Secaucus, New Jersey.

Additional copies of *Mind Your Own Business* may be ordered by sending a check for $18.95 (please add the following for postage and handling: $2.00 for the first copy, $1.00 for each added copy) to:

> MasterMedia Limited
> 17 East 89th Street
> New York, NY 10128
> (212) 260-5600
> (800) 334-8232
> (212) 546-7607 (fax)

Marcy Syms is available for speeches. Please contact MasterMedia's Speakers' Bureau for availability and fee arrangements. Call Tony Colao at (908) 359-1612.

Other MasterMedia Books

THE PREGNANCY AND MOTHERHOOD DIARY: Planning the First Year of Your Second Career, by Susan Schiffer Stautberg. ($12.95 spiralbound)

CITIES OF OPPORTUNITY: Finding the Best Place to Work, Live and Prosper in the 1990's and Beyond, by Dr. John Tepper Marlin. ($13.95 paper, $24.95 cloth)

THE DOLLARS AND SENSE OF DIVORCE, by Dr. Judith Briles. ($10.95 paper)

OUT THE ORGANIZATION: New Career Opportunities for the 1990's, by Madeleine & Robert Swain. ($12.95 paper)

AGING PARENTS AND YOU: A Complete Handbook to Help You Help Your Elders Maintain a Healthy, Productive and Independent Life, by Eugenia Anderson-Ellis. Revised and updated. ($9.95 paper)

CRITICISM IN YOUR LIFE: How to Give It, How to Take It, How to Make It Work for You, by Dr. Deborah Bright. ($17.95 cloth)

BEYOND SUCCESS: How Volunteer Service Can Help You Begin Making a Life Instead of Just a Living, by John F. Raynolds III and Eleanor Raynolds, C.B.E. ($19.95 cloth)

MANAGING IT ALL: Time-Saving Ideas for Career, Family, Relationships, and Self, by Beverly Benz Treuille and Susan Schiffer Stautberg. ($9.95 paper)

YOUR HEALTHY BODY, YOUR HEALTHY LIFE: How to Take Control of Your Medical Destiny, by Donald B. Louria, M.D. Revised and updated. ($12.95 paper)

THE CONFIDENCE FACTOR: How Self-Esteem Can Change Your Life, by Dr. Judith Briles. ($9.95 paper, $18.95 cloth)

THE SOLUTION TO POLLUTION: 101 Things You Can Do to Clean Up Your Environment, by Laurence Sombke. ($7.95 paper)

TAKING CONTROL OF YOUR LIFE: The Secrets of Successful Enterprising Women, by Gail Blanke and Kathleen Walas. ($17.95 cloth)

SIDE-BY-SIDE STRATEGIES: How Two-Career Couples Can Thrive in the Nineties, by Jane Hershey Cuozzo and S. Diane Graham. Published in hardcover as *Power Partners.* ($10.95 paper, $19.95 cloth)

DARE TO CONFRONT! How to Intervene When Someone You Care About Has an Alcohol or Drug Problem, by Bob Wright and Deborah George Wright. ($17.95 cloth)

WORK WITH ME! How to Make the Most of Office Support Staff, by Betsy Lazary. ($9.95 paper)

MANN FOR ALL SEASONS: Wit and Wisdom from The Washington Post's *Judy Mann,* by Judy Mann. ($9.95 paper, $19.95 cloth)

THE SOLUTION TO POLLUTION IN THE WORKPLACE, by Laurence Sombke, Terry M. Robertson, and Elliot M. Kaplan. ($9.95 paper)

THE ENVIRONMENTAL GARDENER: The Solution to Pollution for Lawns and Gardens, by Laurence Sombke. ($8.95 paper)

THE LOYALTY FACTOR: Building Trust in Today's Workplace, by Carol Kinsey Goman, Ph.D.. ($9.95 paper)

DARE TO CHANGE YOUR JOB—AND YOUR LIFE, by Carole Kanchier, Ph.D. ($9.95 paper)

MISS AMERICA: In Pursuit of the Crown, by Ann-Marie Bivans. ($19.95 paper, $27.50 cloth)

POSITIVELY OUTRAGEOUS SERVICE: New and Easy Ways to Win Customers for Life, by T. Scott Gross. ($14.95 paper)

BREATHING SPACE: Living and Working at a Comfortable Pace in a Sped-Up Society, by Jeff Davidson. ($10.95 paper)

TWENTYSOMETHING: Managing and Motivating Today's New Work Force, by Lawrence J. Bradford, Ph.D., and Claire Raines, M.A. ($22.95 cloth)

REAL LIFE 101: The Graduate's Guide to Survival, by Susan Kleinman. ($9.95 paper)

BALANCING ACTS! Juggling Love, Work, Family, and Recreation, by Susan Schiffer Stautberg and Marcia L. Worthing. ($12.95 paper)

REAL BEAUTY... REAL WOMEN: A Handbook for Making the Best of Your Own Good Looks, by Kathleen Walas, International Beauty and Fashion Director of Avon Products. ($19.50 paper)

THE LIVING HEART BRAND NAME SHOPPER'S GUIDE, by Michael E. DeBakey, M.D., Antonio M. Gotto, Jr., M.D., D.Phil., Lynne W. Scott, M.A., R.D./L.D., and John P. Foreyt, Ph.D. ($12.50 paper)

MANAGING YOUR CHILD'S DIABETES, by Robert Wood Johnson IV, Sale Johnson, Casey Johnson, and Susan Kleinman. ($10.95 paper)

STEP FORWARD: Sexual Harassment in the Workplace, What You Need to Know, by Susan L. Webb. ($9.95 paper)

A TEEN'S GUIDE TO BUSINESS: The Secrets to a Successful Enterprise, by Linda Menzies, Oren S. Jenkins, and Rickell R. Fisher. ($7.95 paper)

GLORIOUS ROOTS: Recipes for Healthy, Tasty Vegetables, by Laurence Sombke. ($12.95 paper)

THE OUTDOOR WOMAN: A Handbook to Adventure, by Patricia Hubbard and Stan Wass. ($14.95 paper)

FLIGHT PLAN FOR LIVING: The Art of Self-Encouragement, by Patrick O'Dooley. ($17.95 cloth)

HOW TO GET WHAT YOU WANT FROM ALMOST ANYBODY, by T. Scott Gross. ($9.95 paper)

FINANCIAL SAVVY FOR WOMEN: A Money Book for Women of All Ages, by Dr. Judith Briles. ($14.95 paper)

TEAMBUILT: Making Teamwork Work, by Mark Sanborn. ($19.95 cloth)

THE BIG APPLE BUSINESS AND PLEASURE GUIDE: 501 Ways to Work Smarter, Play Harder, and Live Better in New York City, by Muriel Siebert and Susan Kleinman. ($9.95 paper)